MARK CRILLEY

VOLUME FOUR

Issues 19 ~ 25
"The Story Tree"

SIRIUS ENTERTAINMENT   **DOVER, N. J.**

This book is dedicated to
Matthew Crilley

SIRIUS

PUBLISHER
ROBB HORAN

ART DIRECTION
JOSEPH MICHAEL LINSNER

MANAGING EDITOR
MARK BELLIS

PRESIDENT
LAWRENCE SALAMONE

AKIKO VOLUME FOUR "The Story Tree." FEBRUARY, 2000. FIRST PRINTING
PUBLISHED BY SIRIUS ENTERTAINMENT, INC. LAWRENCE SALAMONE, PRESIDENT.
ROBB HORAN, PUBLISHER, JOSEPH MICHAEL LINSNER, ART DIRECTOR.
CORRESPONDENCE: P.O. BOX 834, DOVER, N.J. 07802. AKIKO IS © 2000 MARK CRILLEY
SIRIUS & THE DOGSTAR LOGO ARE TM AND © SIRIUS ENTERTAINMENT, INC. ALL RIGHTS RESERVED.
ANY SIMILARITY TO PERSONS LIVING OR DEAD IS PURELY COINCIDENTAL.
CAUTION: FILLING MAY BE HOT

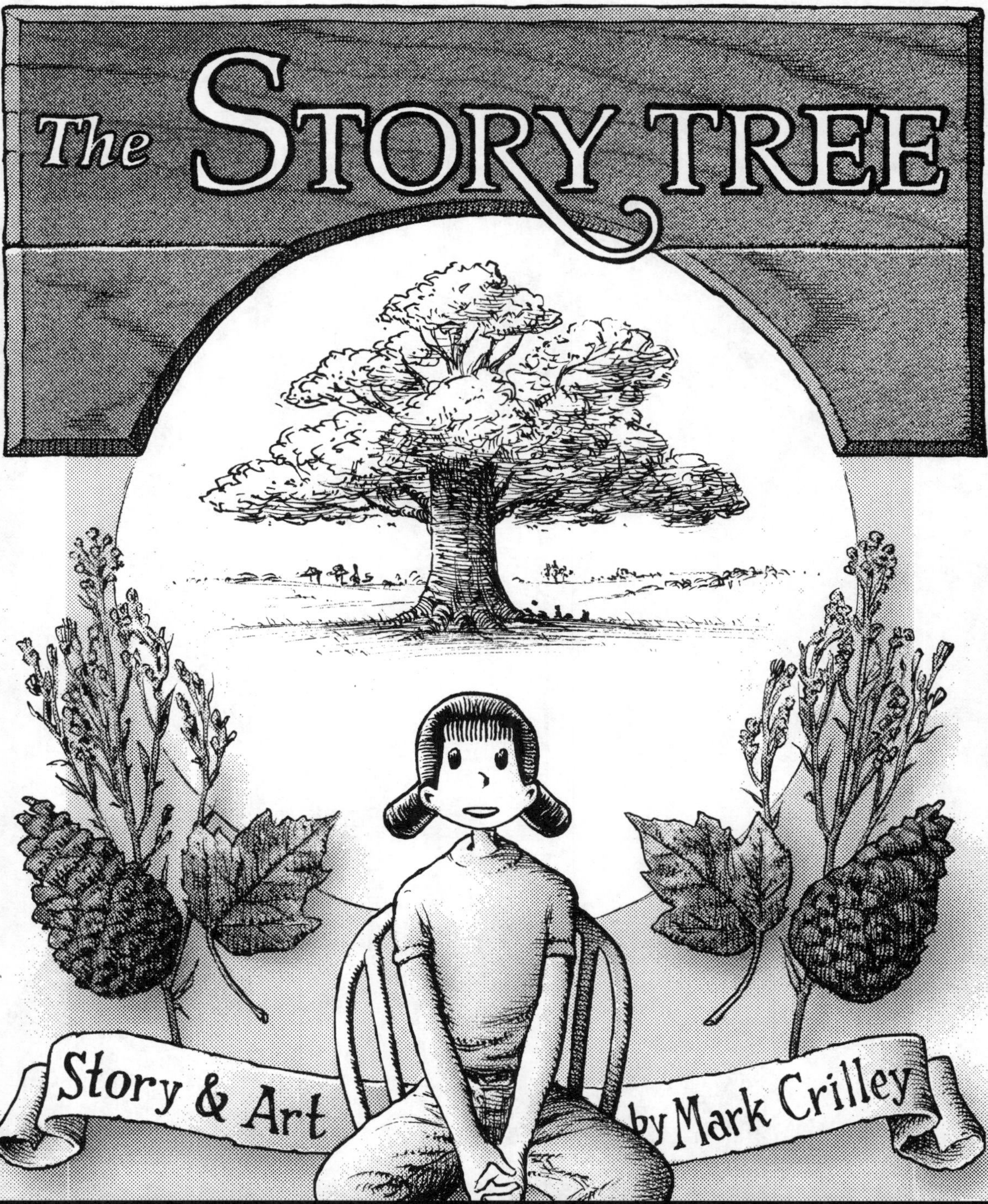
The STORY TREE
Story & Art
by Mark Crilley

My name is Akiko. Today I want to tell you about the day my friends from the planet Smoo came to visit me here on earth. I was happy to see them, but I knew we had to be careful not to be seen by too many people.

So we held a meeting in my bedroom and decided to go way out to the countryside where no one could bother us. Then for the rest of the day all we did was just sit around telling stories under this great, big tree...

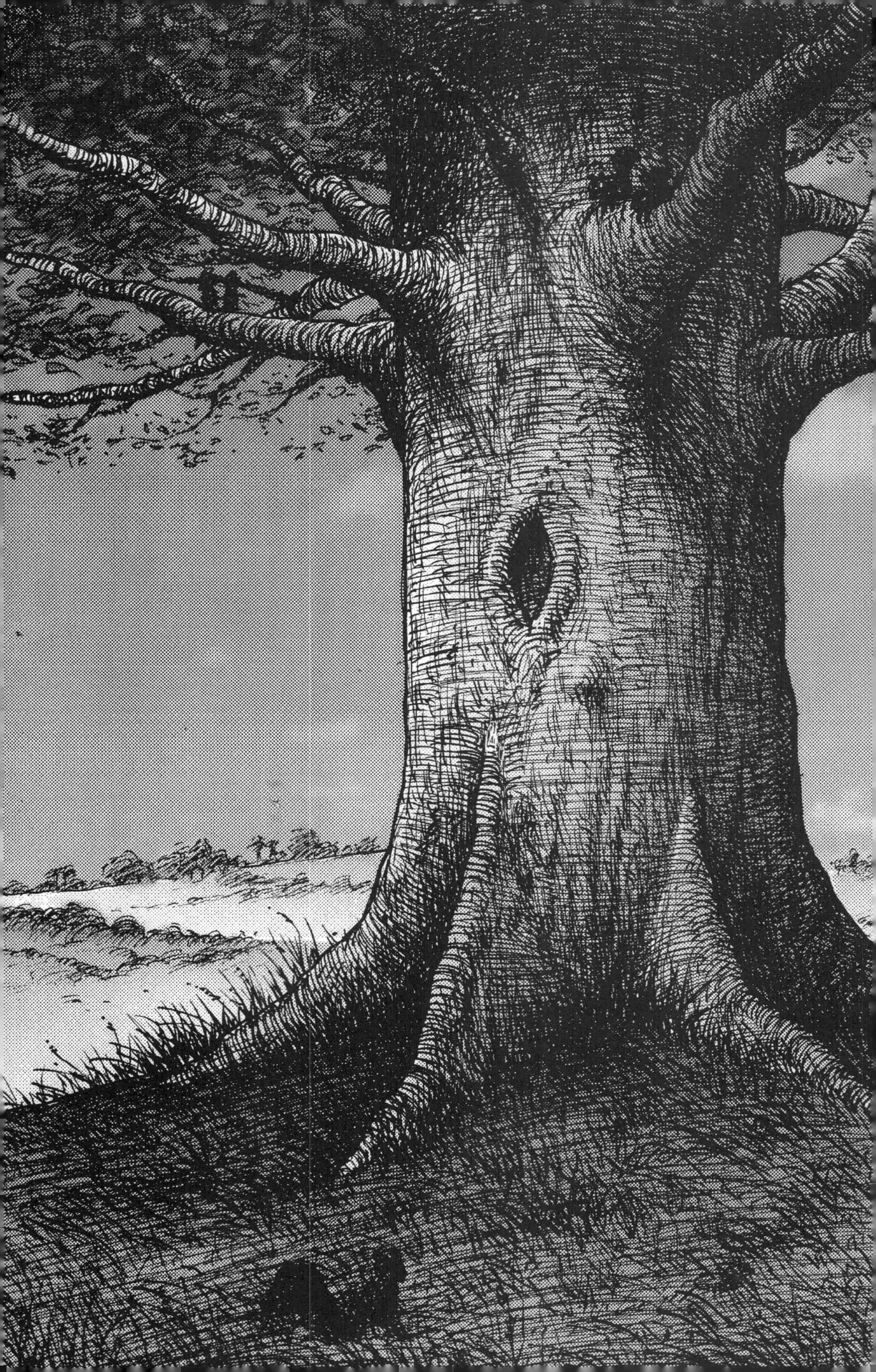

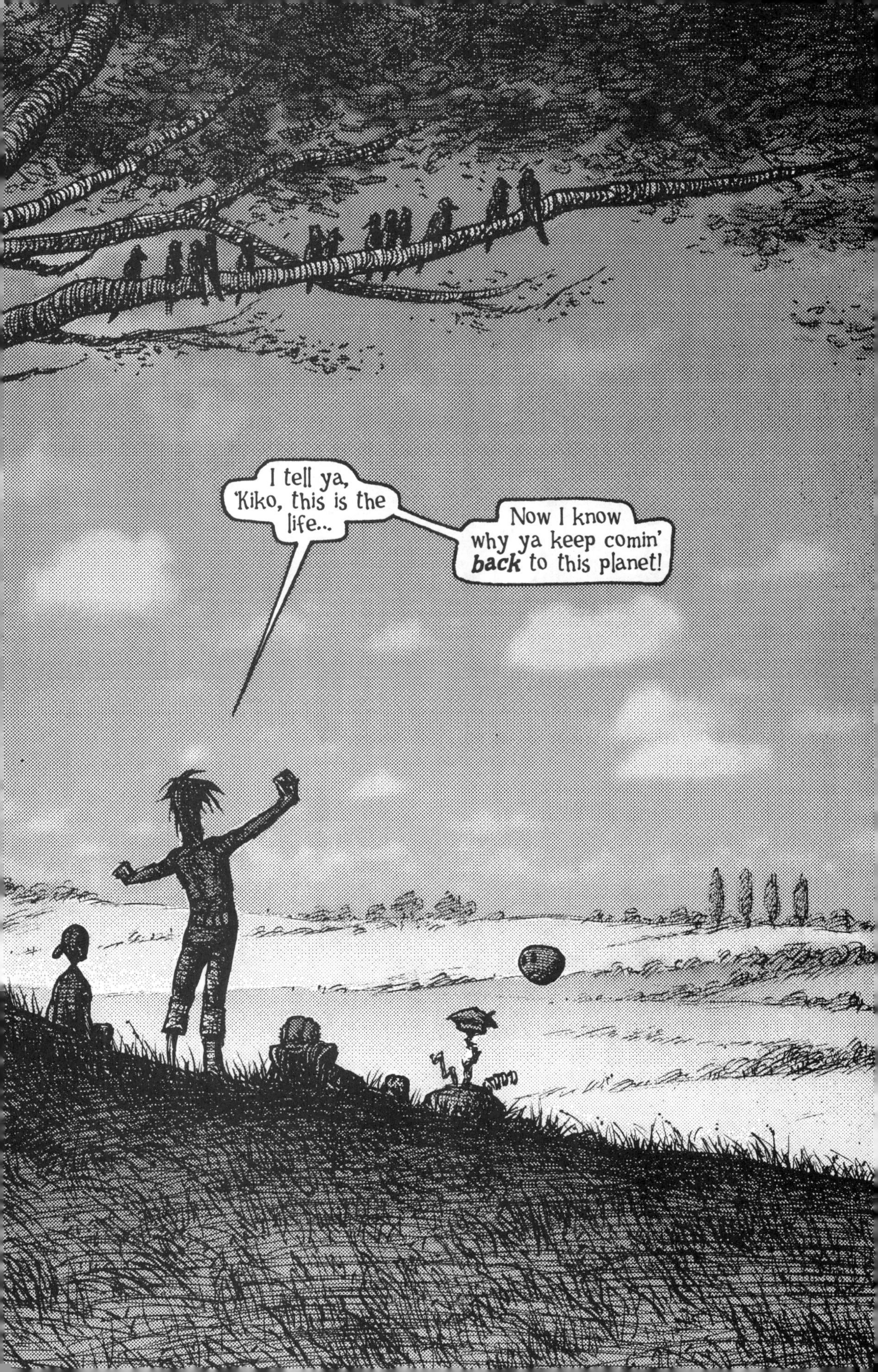
I tell ya, 'Kiko, this is the life...
Now I know why ya keep comin' ***back*** to this planet!

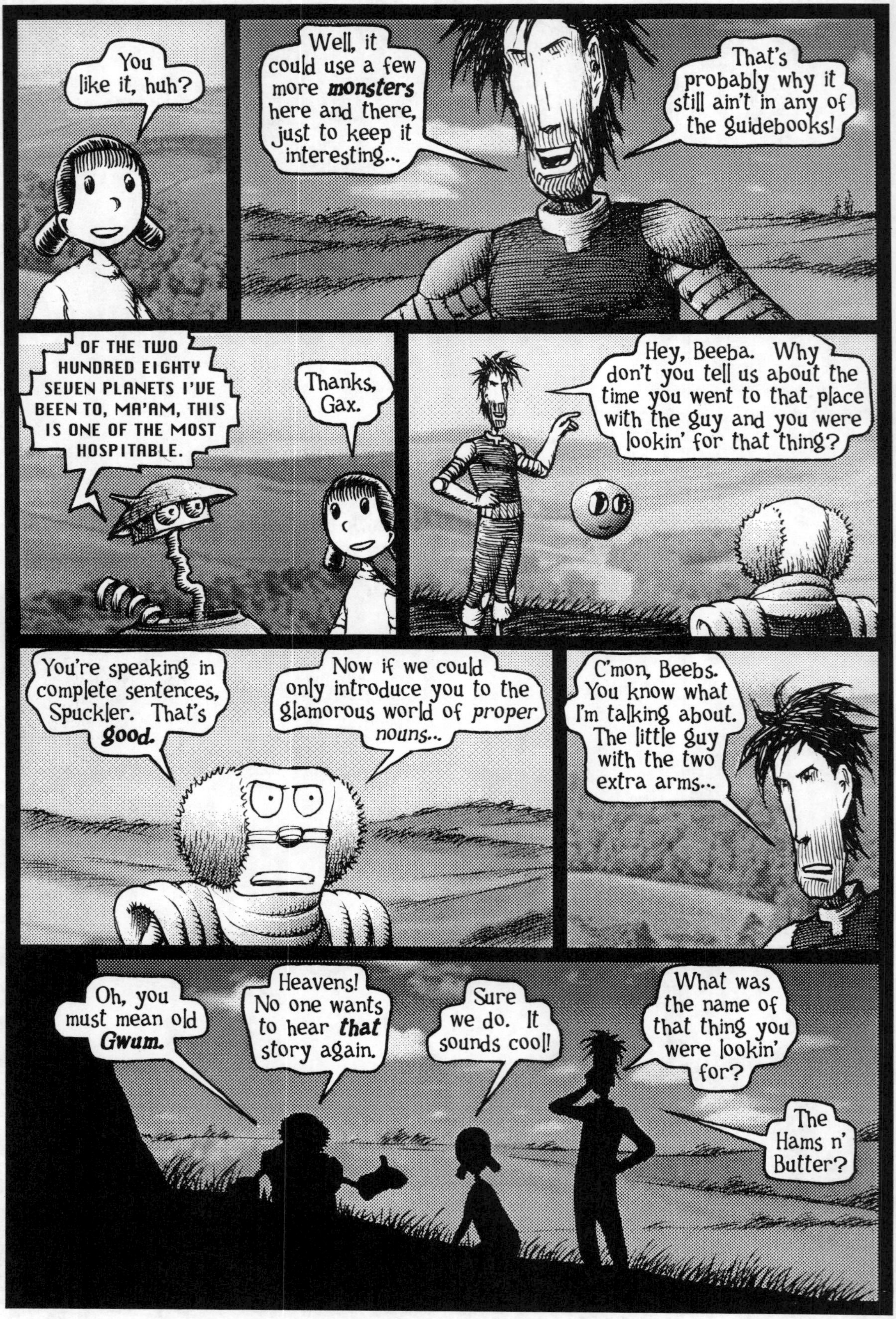
You like it, huh?
Well, it could use a few more **monsters** here and there, just to keep it interesting...
That's probably why it still ain't in any of the guidebooks!
OF THE TWO HUNDRED EIGHTY SEVEN PLANETS I'VE BEEN TO, MA'AM, THIS IS ONE OF THE MOST HOSPITABLE.
Thanks, Gax.
Hey, Beeba. Why don't you tell us about the time you went to that place with the guy and you were lookin' for that thing?
You're speaking in complete sentences, Spuckler. That's **good.**
Now if we could only introduce you to the glamorous world of *proper* nouns...
C'mon, Beebs. You know what I'm talking about. The little guy with the two extra arms...
Oh, you must mean old **Gwum.**
Heavens! No one wants to hear **that** story again.
Sure we do. It sounds cool!
What was the name of that thing you were lookin' for?
The Hams n' Butter?

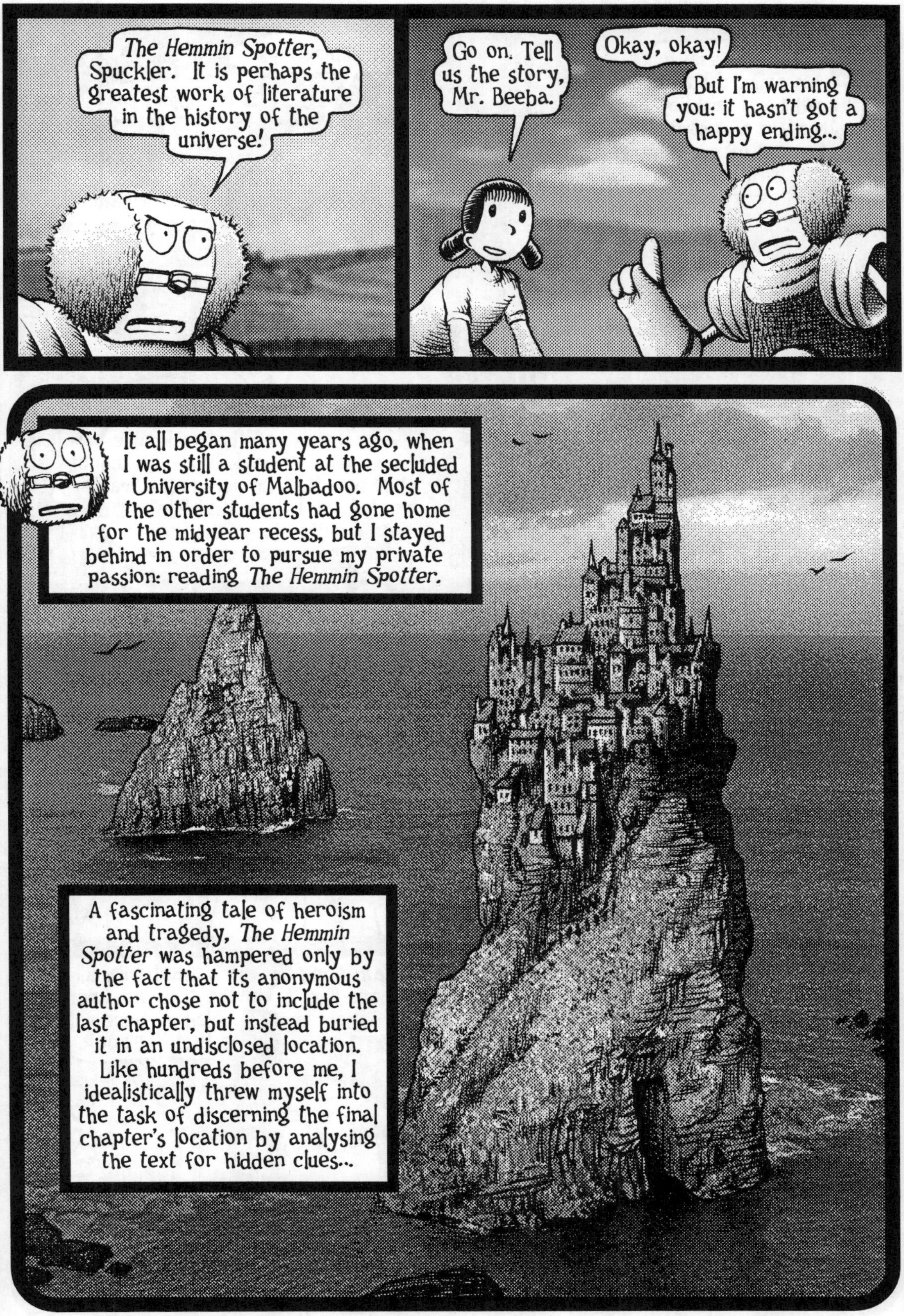

The Hemmin Spotter, Spuckler. It is perhaps the greatest work of literature in the history of the universe!
Go on. Tell us the story, Mr. Beeba.
Okay, okay!
But I'm warning you: it hasn't got a happy ending...
It all began many years ago, when I was still a student at the secluded University of Malbadoo. Most of the other students had gone home for the midyear recess, but I stayed behind in order to pursue my private passion: reading The Hemmin Spotter.
A fascinating tale of heroism and tragedy, The Hemmin Spotter was hampered only by the fact that its anonymous author chose not to include the last chapter, but instead buried it in an undisclosed location. Like hundreds before me, I idealistically threw myself into the task of discerning the final chapter's location by analysing the text for hidden clues...

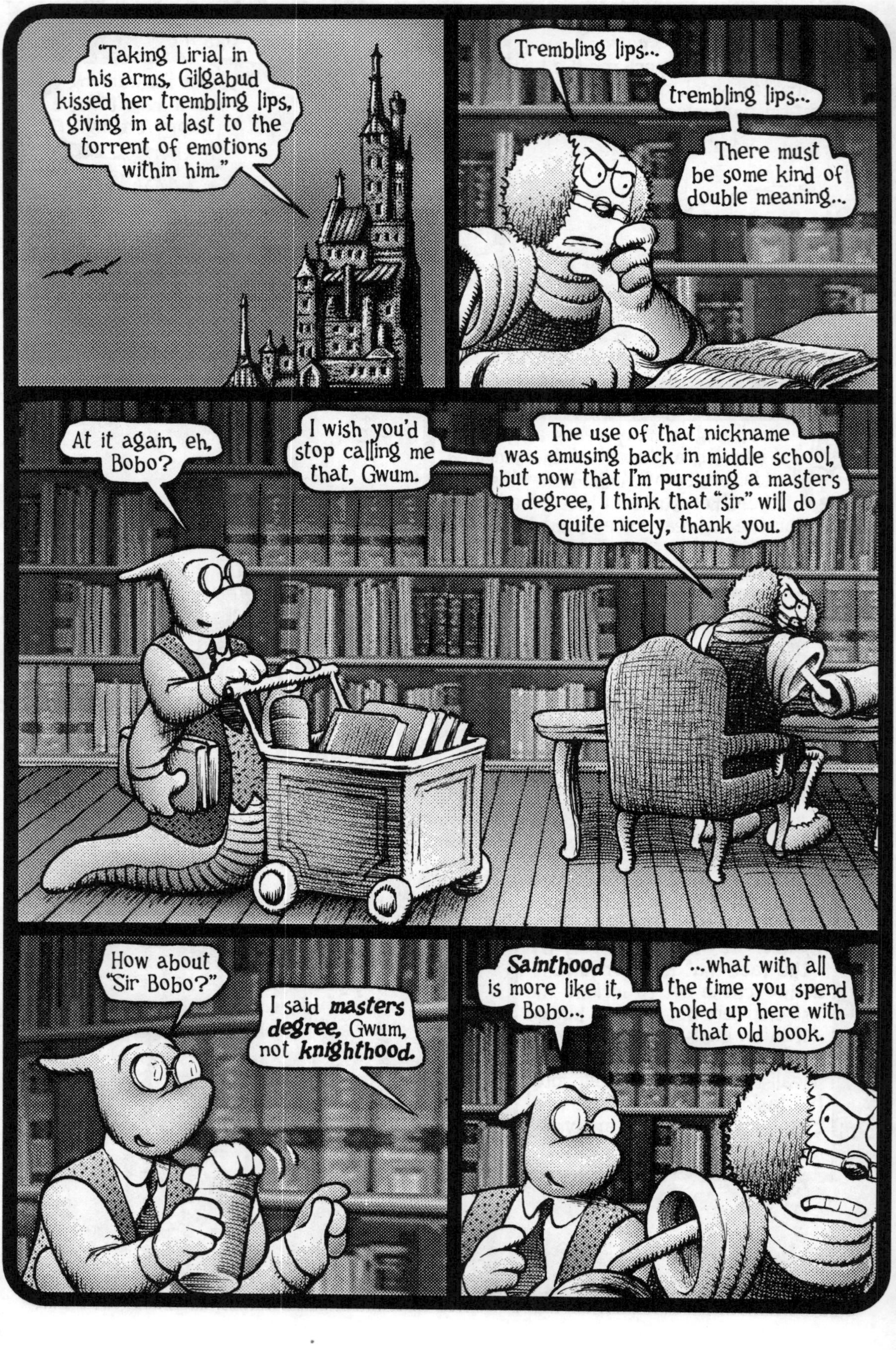
"Taking Lirial in his arms, Gilgabud kissed her trembling lips, giving in at last to the torrent of emotions within him."
Trembling lips...
trembling lips...
There must be some kind of double meaning...
At it again, eh, Bobo?
I wish you'd stop calling me that, Gwum.
The use of that nickname was amusing back in middle school, but now that I'm pursuing a masters degree, I think that "sir" will do quite nicely, thank you.
How about "Sir Bobo?"
I said **masters degree,** Gwum, not **knighthood.**
Sainthood is more like it, Bobo...
...what with all the time you spend holed up here with that old book.

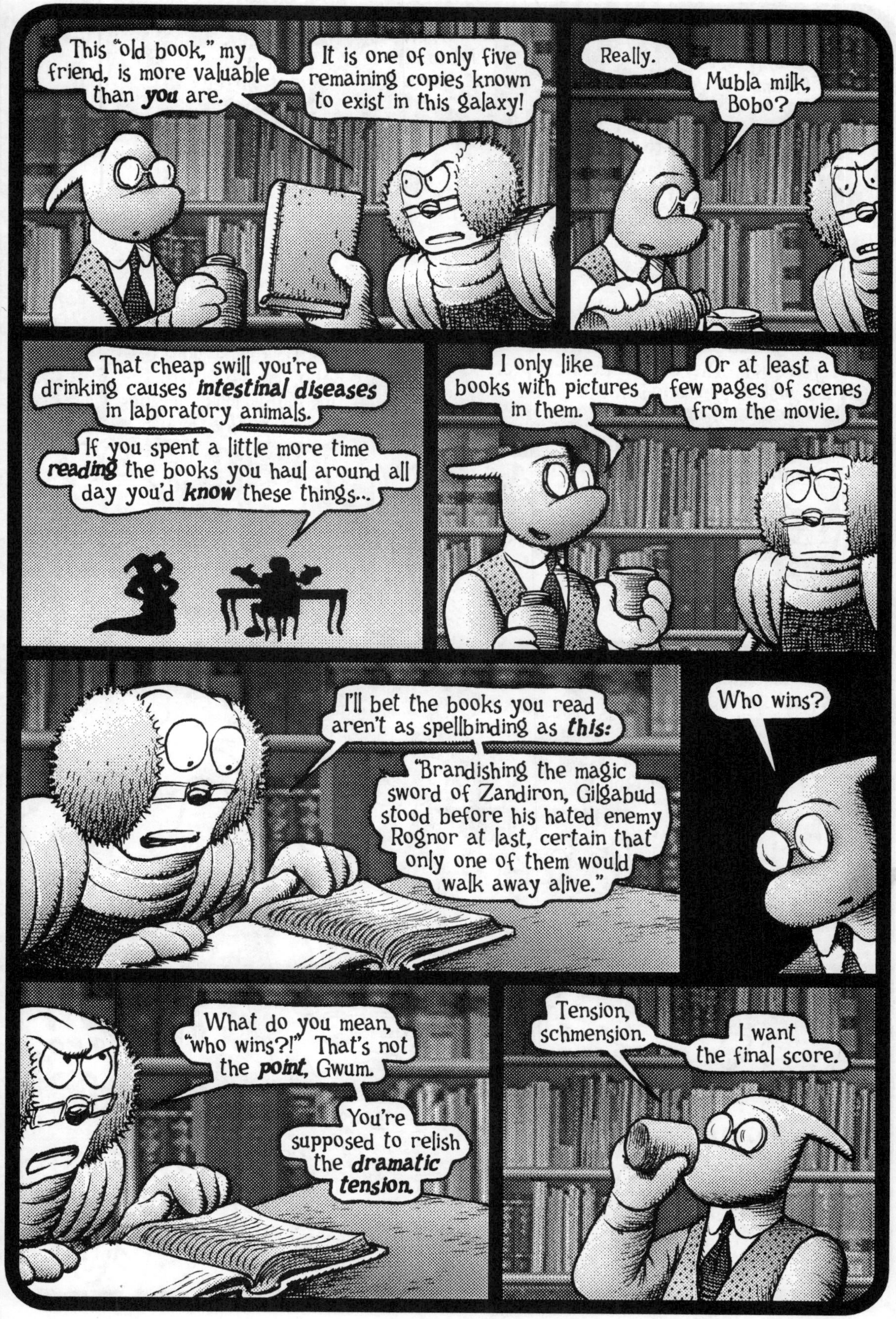
This "old book," my friend, is more valuable than *you* are.
It is one of only five remaining copies known to exist in this galaxy!
Really.
Mubla milk, Bobo?
That cheap swill you're drinking causes *intestinal diseases* in laboratory animals.
If you spent a little more time *reading* the books you haul around all day you'd *know* these things...
I only like books with pictures in them.
Or at least a few pages of scenes from the movie.
I'll bet the books you read aren't as spellbinding as *this:*
"Brandishing the magic sword of Zandiron, Gilgabud stood before his hated enemy Rognor at last, certain that only one of them would walk away alive."
Who wins?
What do you mean, "who wins?!" That's not the *point*, Gwum.
You're supposed to relish the *dramatic tension.*
Tension, schmension.
I want the final score.

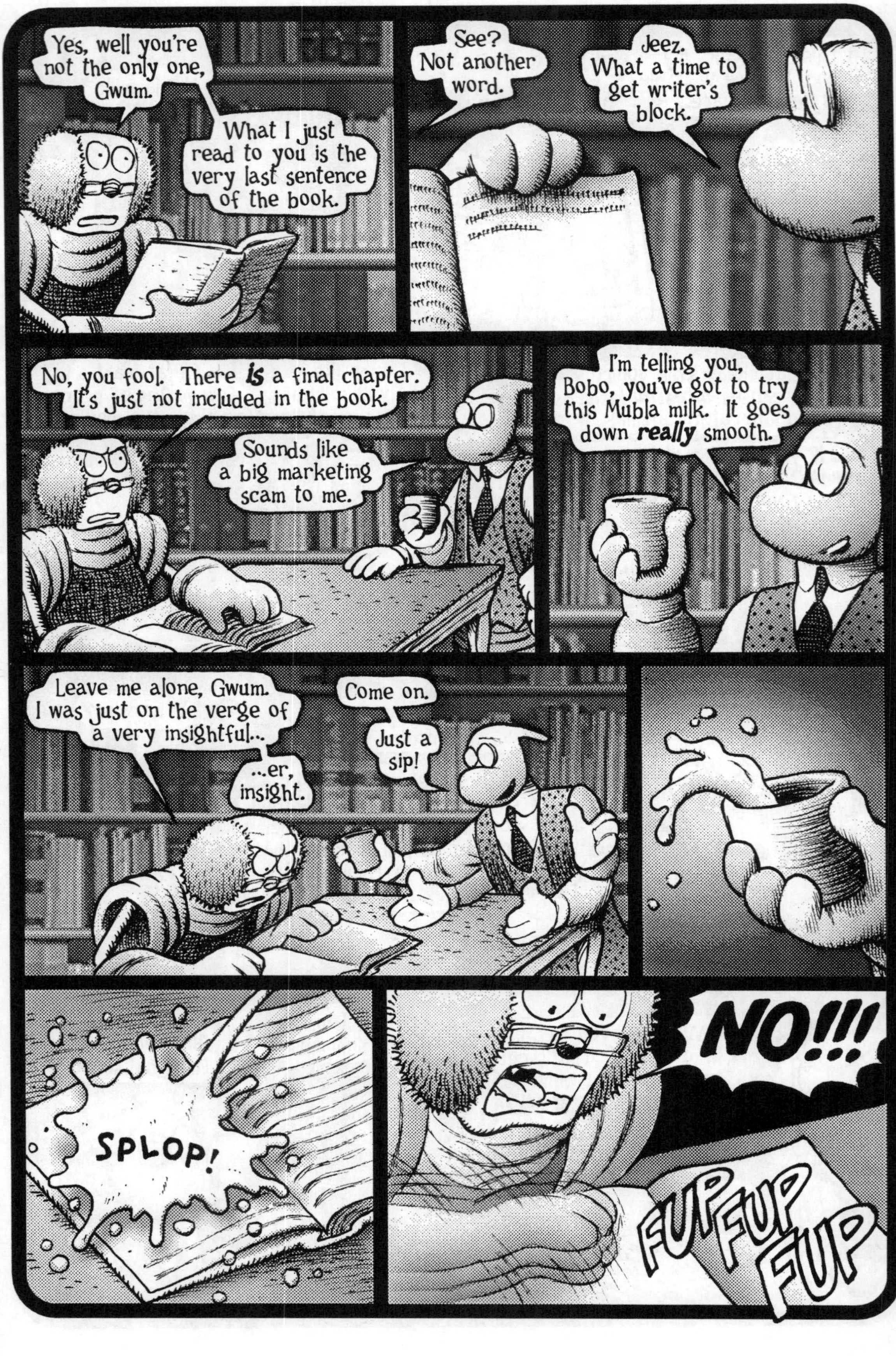
Yes, well you're not the only one, Gwum.
What I just read to you is the very last sentence of the book.
See? Not another word.
Jeez. What a time to get writer's block.
No, you fool. There **is** a final chapter. It's just not included in the book.
Sounds like a big marketing scam to me.
I'm telling you, Bobo, you've got to try this Mubla milk. It goes down **really** smooth.
Leave me alone, Gwum. I was just on the verge of a very insightful...
...er, insight.
Come on.
Just a sip!
SPLOP!
NO!!!
FUP FUP FUP

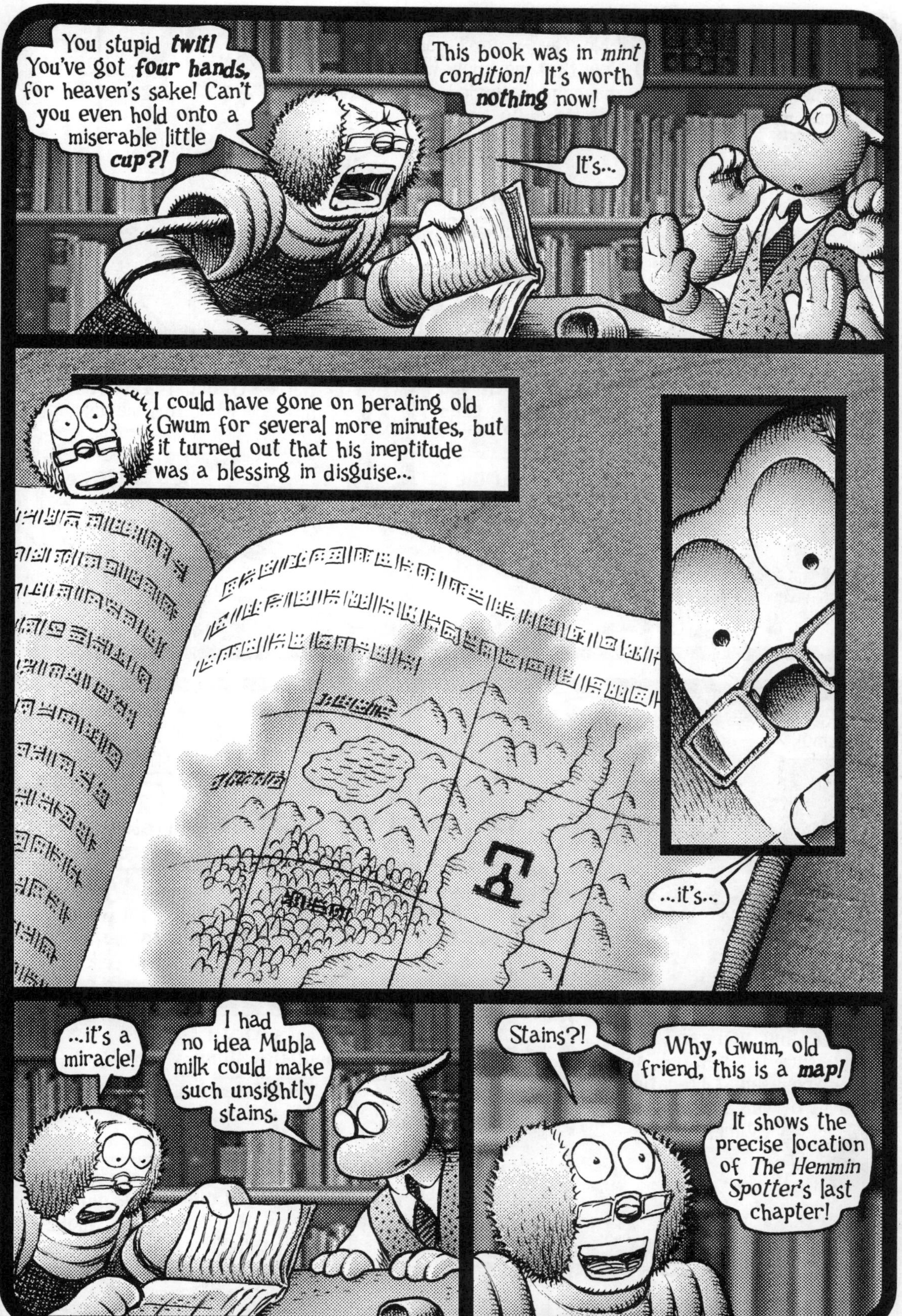
You stupid *twit!* You've got **four hands,** for heaven's sake! Can't you even hold onto a miserable little *cup?!*
This book was in *mint condition!* It's worth ***nothing*** now!
It's...
I could have gone on berating old Gwum for several more minutes, but it turned out that his ineptitude was a blessing in disguise...
...it's...
...it's a miracle!
I had no idea Mubla milk could make such unsightly stains.
Stains?!
Why, Gwum, old friend, this is a ***map!***
It shows the precise location of *The Hemmin Spotter*'s last chapter!

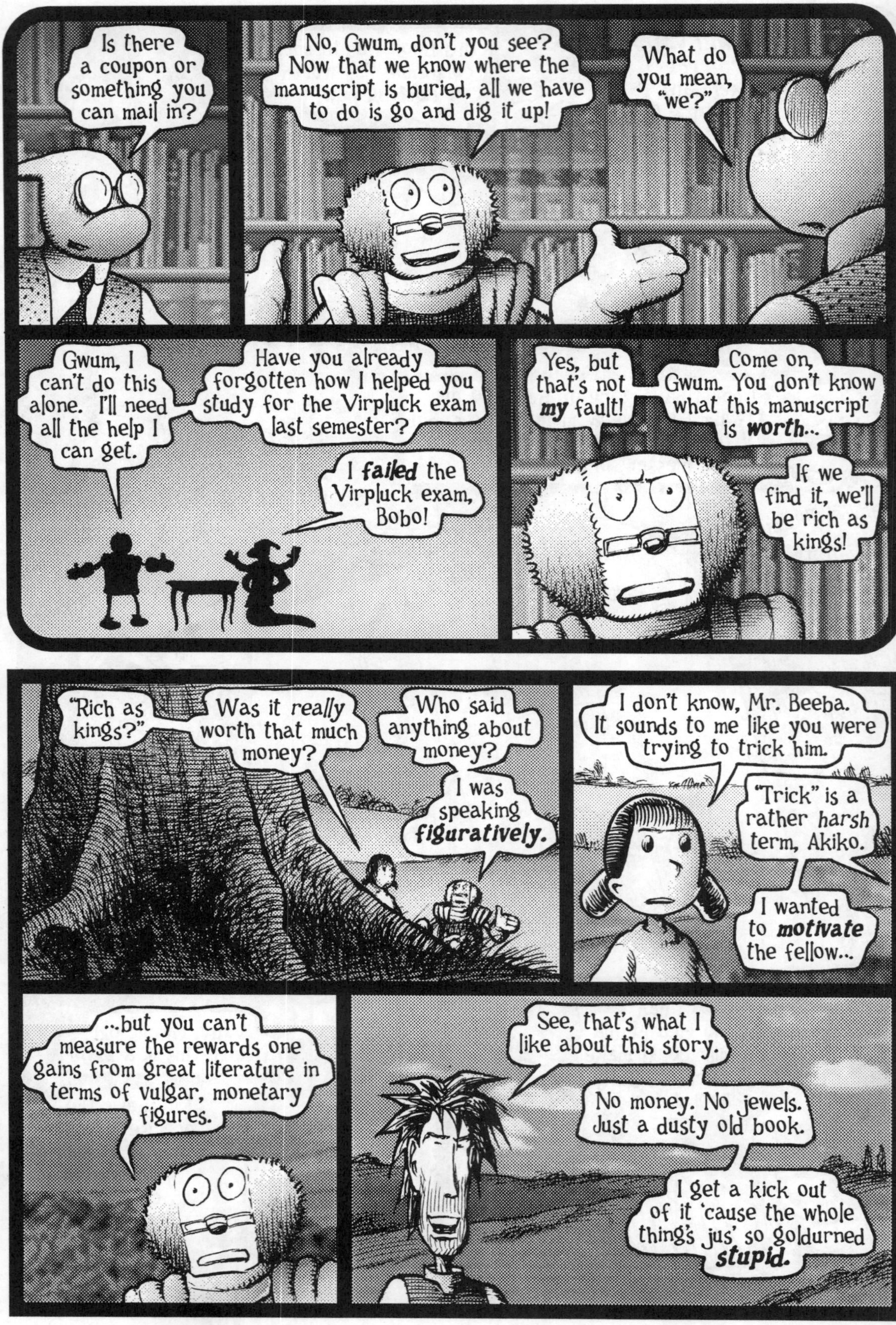
Is there a coupon or something you can mail in?
No, Gwum, don't you see? Now that we know where the manuscript is buried, all we have to do is go and dig it up!
What do you mean, "we?"
Gwum, I can't do this alone. I'll need all the help I can get.
Have you already forgotten how I helped you study for the Virpluck exam last semester?
I **failed** the Virpluck exam, Bobo!
Yes, but that's not **my** fault!
Come on, Gwum. You don't know what this manuscript is **worth**...
If we find it, we'll be rich as kings!
"Rich as kings?"
Was it *really* worth that much money?
Who said anything about money?
I was speaking **figuratively.**
I don't know, Mr. Beeba. It sounds to me like you were trying to trick him.
"Trick" is a rather *harsh* term, Akiko.
I wanted to **motivate** the fellow...
...but you can't measure the rewards one gains from great literature in terms of vulgar, monetary figures.
See, that's what I like about this story.
No money. No jewels. Just a dusty old book.
I get a kick out of it 'cause the whole thing's jus' so goldurned **stupid.**

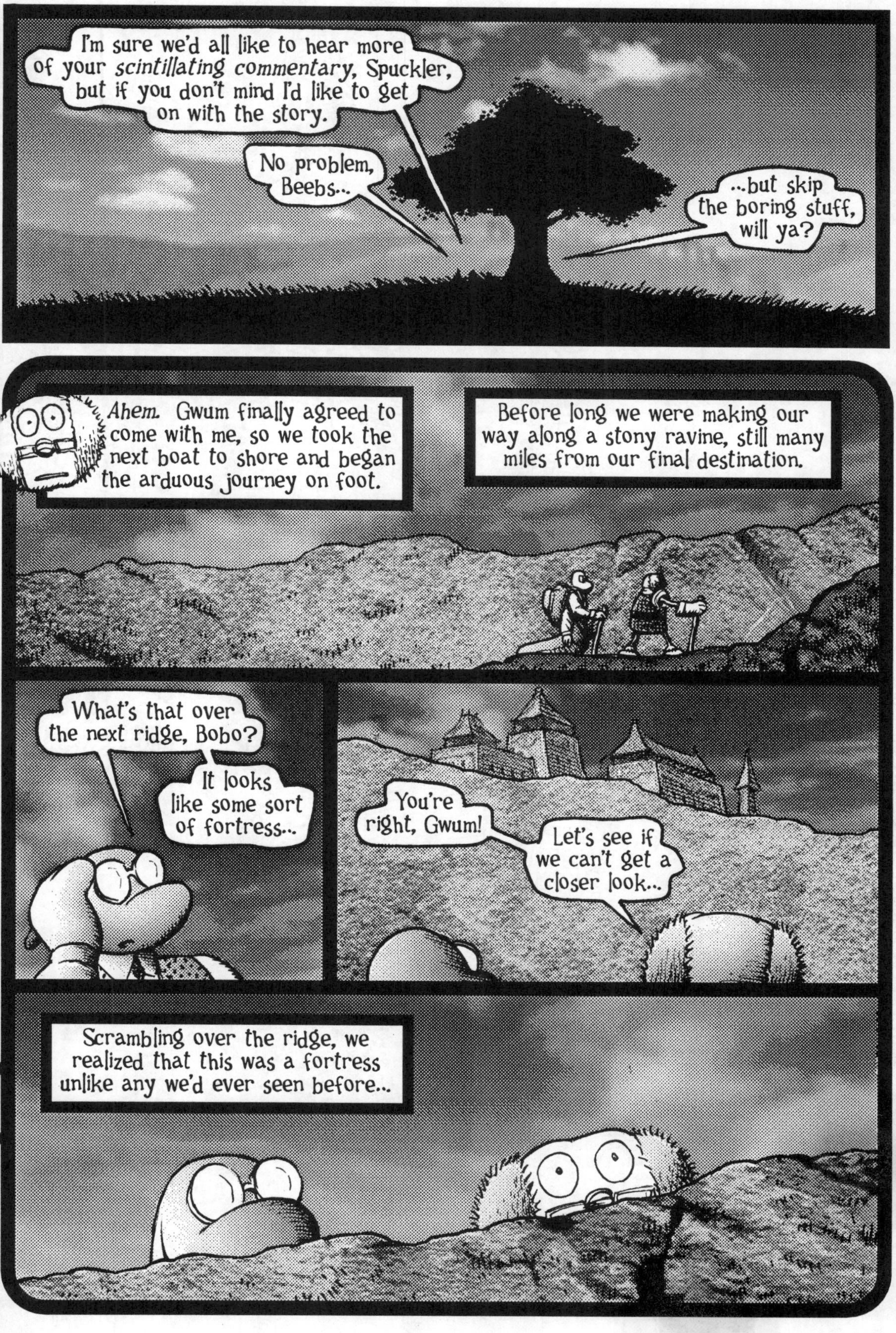
I'm sure we'd all like to hear more of your *scintillating commentary,* Spuckler, but if you don't mind I'd like to get on with the story.
No problem, Beebs...
...but skip the boring stuff, will ya?
Ahem. Gwum finally agreed to come with me, so we took the next boat to shore and began the arduous journey on foot.
Before long we were making our way along a stony ravine, still many miles from our final destination.
What's that over the next ridge, Bobo?
It looks like some sort of fortress...
You're right, Gwum!
Let's see if we can't get a closer look...
Scrambling over the ridge, we realized that this was a fortress unlike any we'd ever seen before...

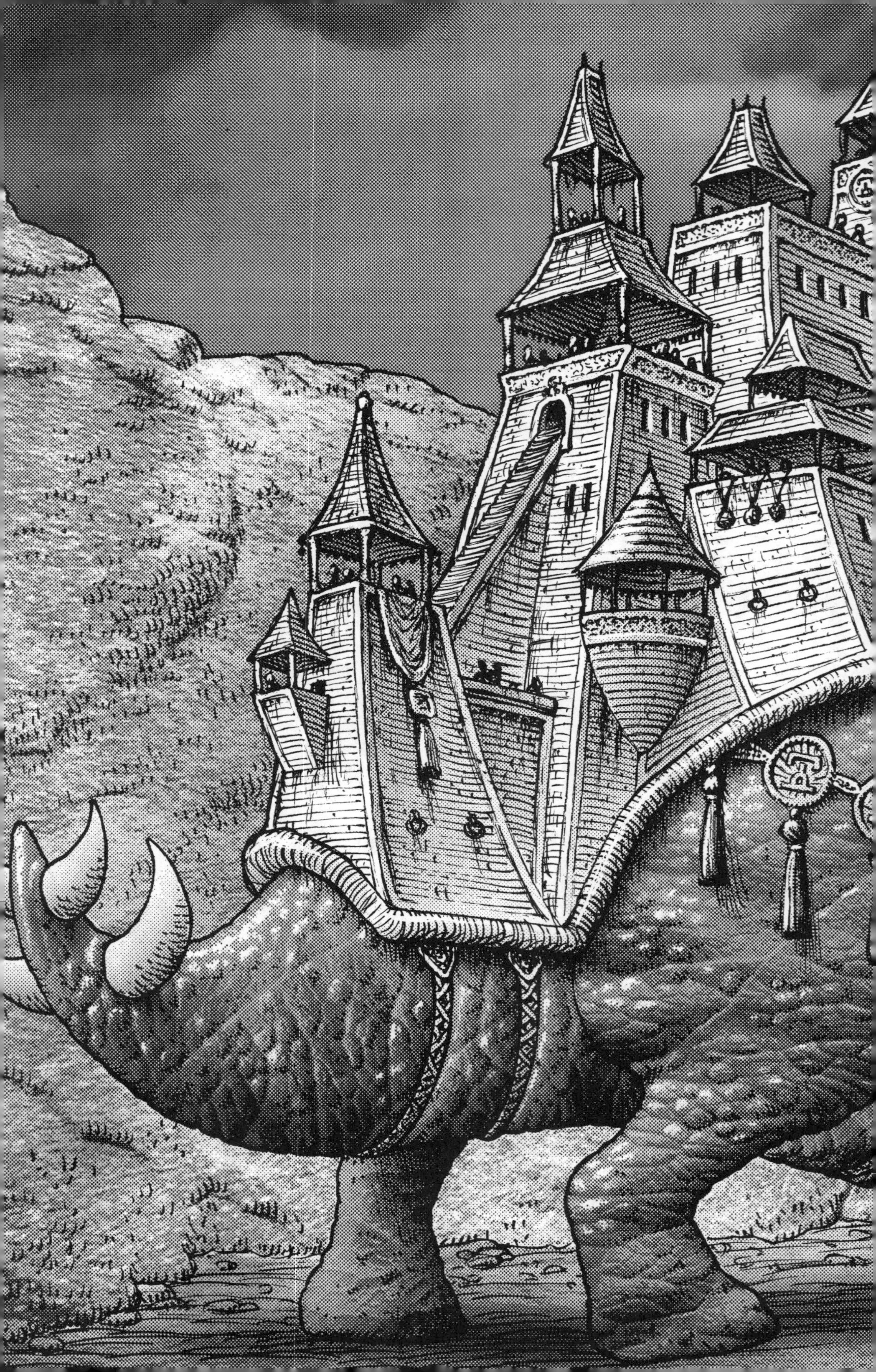

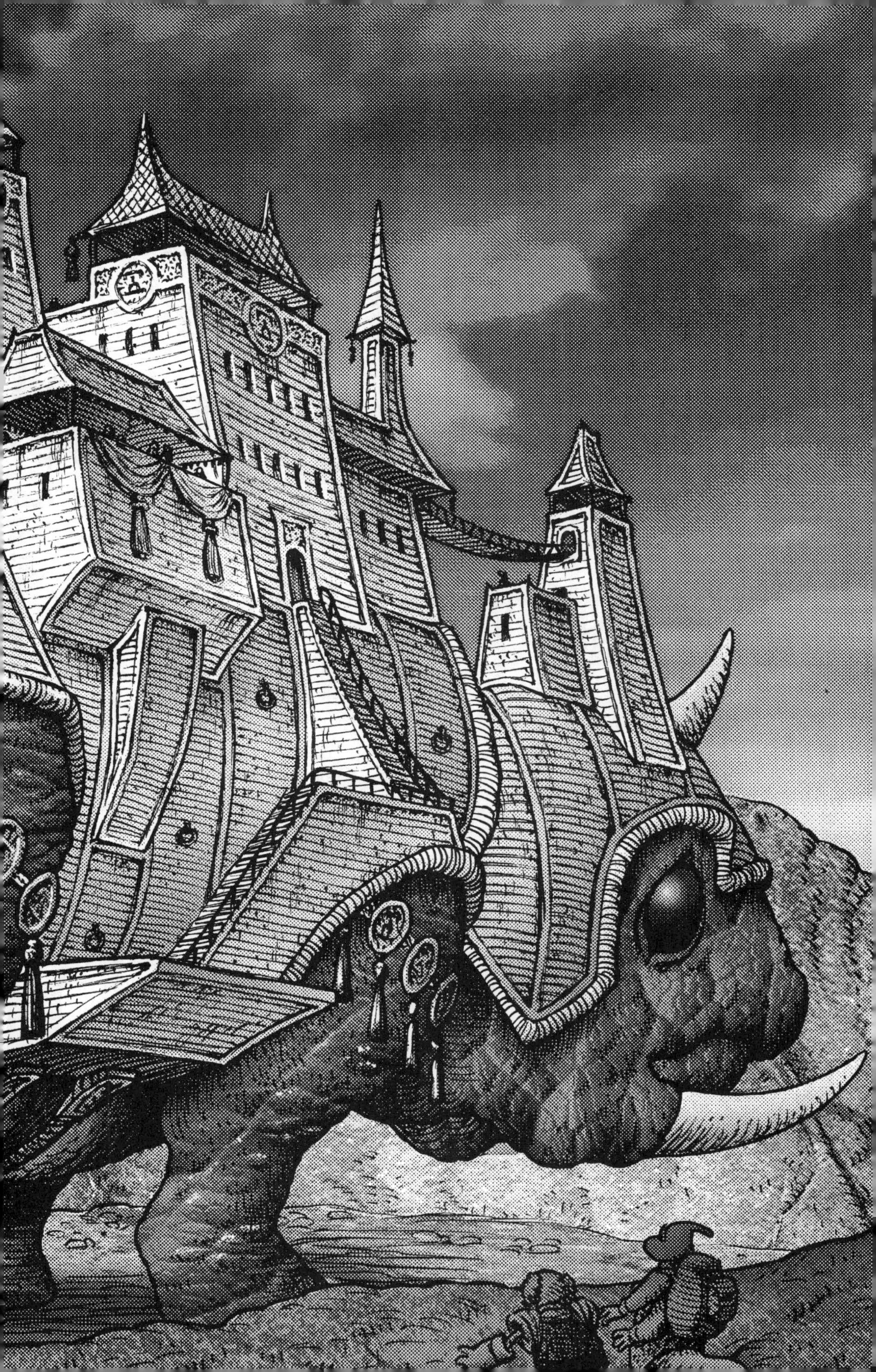

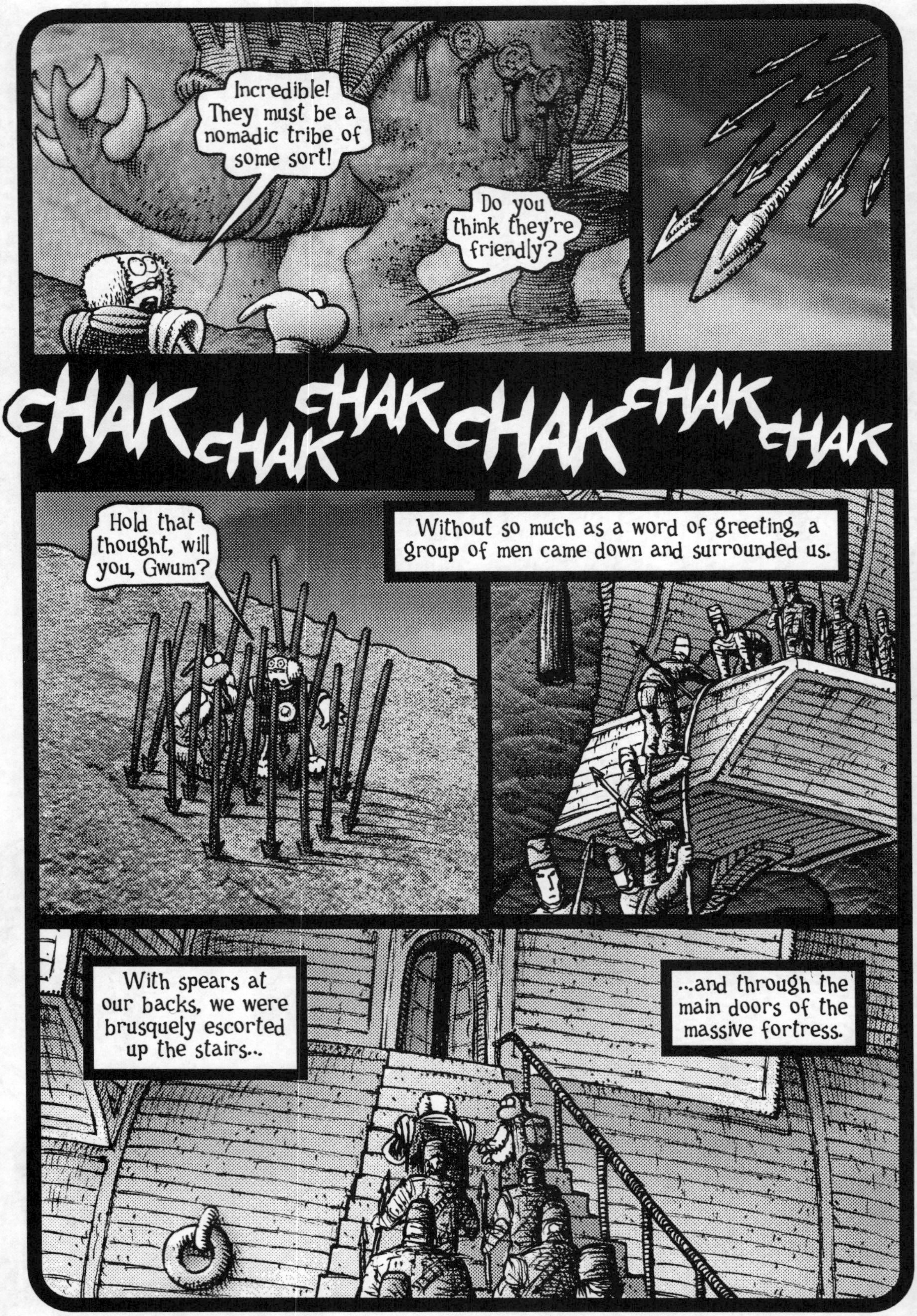

Incredible! They must be a nomadic tribe of some sort!
Do you think they're friendly?
CHAK CHAK CHAK CHAK CHAK CHAK
Hold that thought, will you, Gwum?
Without so much as a word of greeting, a group of men came down and surrounded us.
With spears at our backs, we were brusquely escorted up the stairs...
...and through the main doors of the massive fortress.

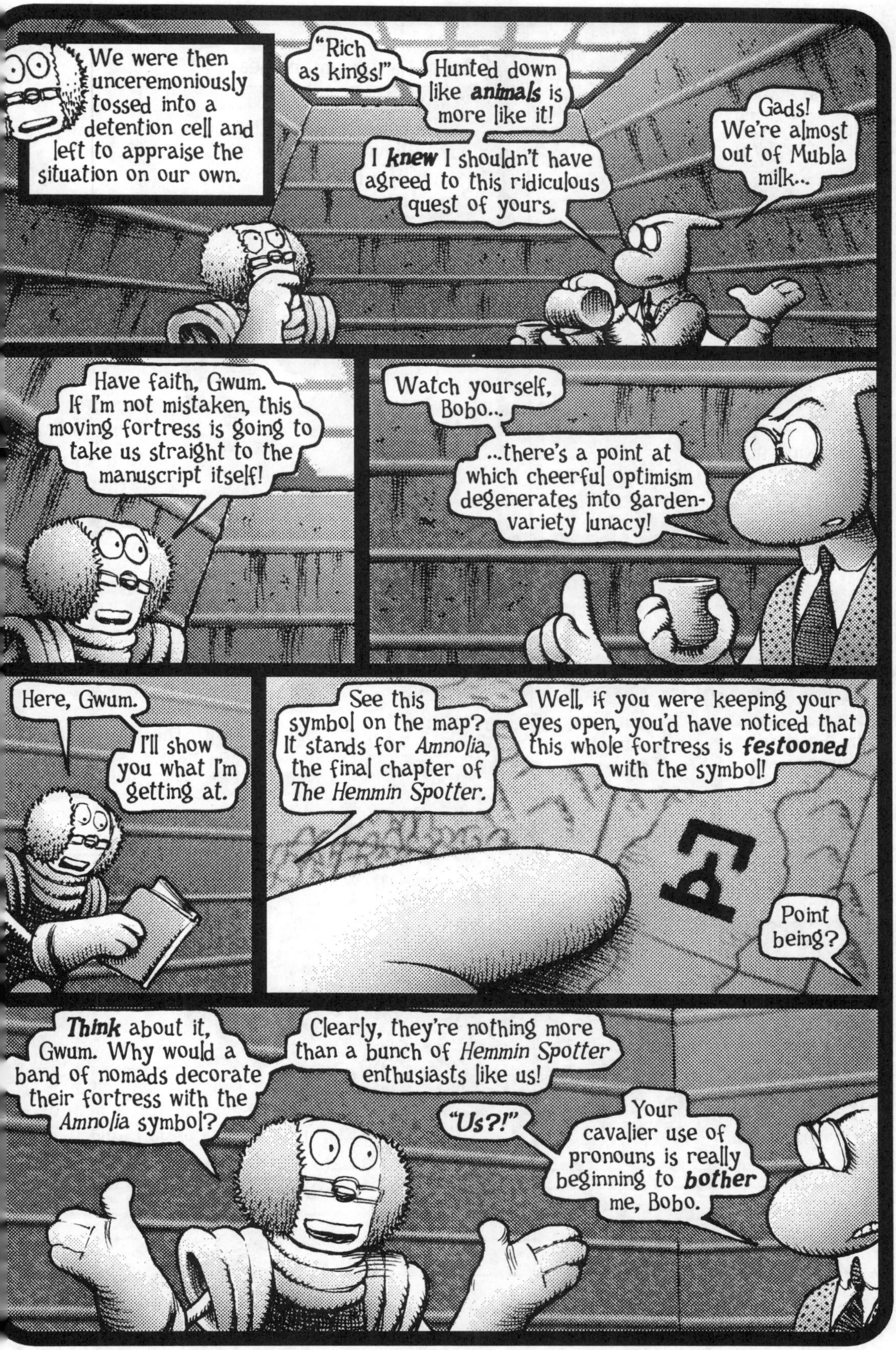

We were then unceremoniously tossed into a detention cell and left to appraise the situation on our own.
"Rich as kings!"
Hunted down like **animals** is more like it!
I **knew** I shouldn't have agreed to this ridiculous quest of yours.
Gads! We're almost out of Mubla milk...
Have faith, Gwum. If I'm not mistaken, this moving fortress is going to take us straight to the manuscript itself!
Watch yourself, Bobo...
...there's a point at which cheerful optimism degenerates into garden-variety lunacy!
Here, Gwum.
I'll show you what I'm getting at.
See this symbol on the map? It stands for *Amnolia*, the final chapter of *The Hemmin Spotter*.
Well, if you were keeping your eyes open, you'd have noticed that this whole fortress is ***festooned*** with the symbol!
Point being?
Think about it, Gwum. Why would a band of nomads decorate their fortress with the *Amnolia* symbol?
Clearly, they're nothing more than a bunch of *Hemmin Spotter* enthusiasts like us!
"Us?!"
Your cavalier use of pronouns is really beginning to ***bother*** me, Bobo.

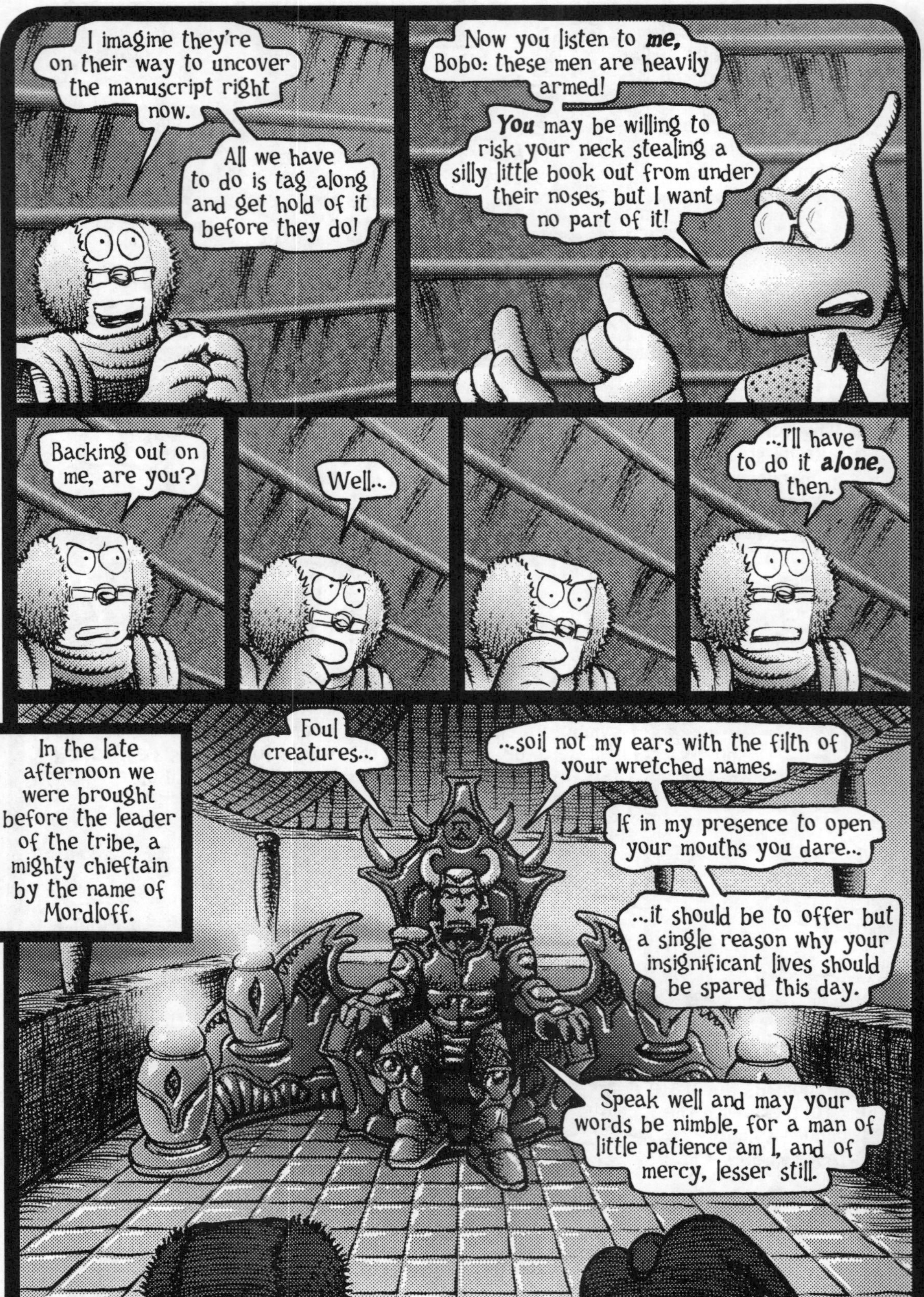

I imagine they're on their way to uncover the manuscript right now.
All we have to do is tag along and get hold of it before they do!
Now you listen to **me,** Bobo: these men are heavily armed!
You may be willing to risk your neck stealing a silly little book out from under their noses, but I want no part of it!
Backing out on me, are you?
Well...
...I'll have to do it ***alone,*** then.
In the late afternoon we were brought before the leader of the tribe, a mighty chieftain by the name of Mordloff.
Foul creatures...
...soil not my ears with the filth of your wretched names.
If in my presence to open your mouths you dare...
...it should be to offer but a single reason why your insignificant lives should be spared this day.
Speak well and may your words be nimble, for a man of little patience am I, and of mercy, lesser still.

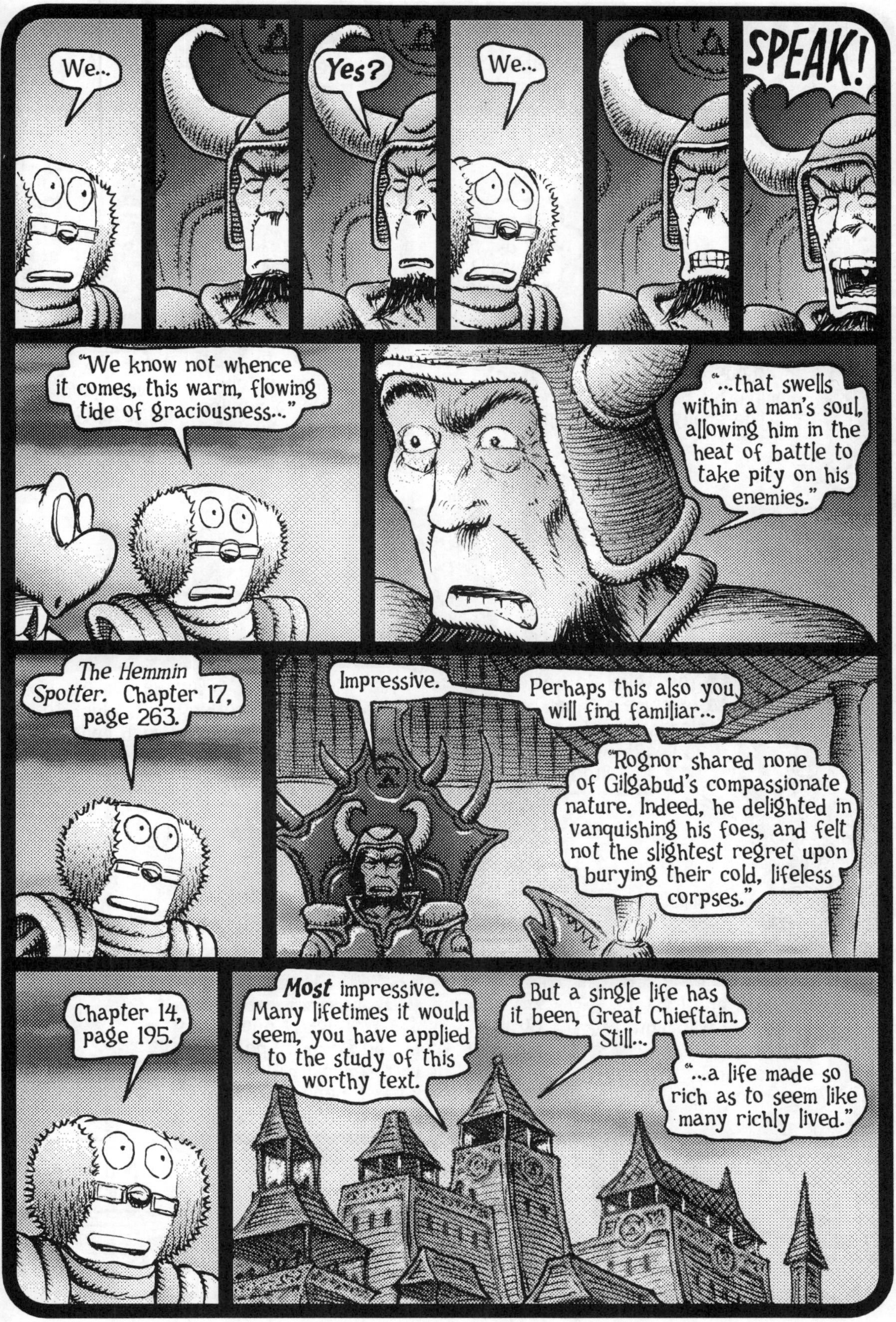
We...
Yes?
We...
SPEAK!
"We know not whence it comes, this warm, flowing tide of graciousness..."
"...that swells within a man's soul, allowing him in the heat of battle to take pity on his enemies."
The Hemmin Spotter. Chapter 17, page 263.
Impressive.
Perhaps this also you will find familiar...
"Rognor shared none of Gilgabud's compassionate nature. Indeed, he delighted in vanquishing his foes, and felt not the slightest regret upon burying their cold, lifeless corpses."
Chapter 14, page 195.
Most impressive. Many lifetimes it would seem, you have applied to the study of this worthy text.
But a single life has it been, Great Chieftain. Still...
"...a life made so rich as to seem like many richly lived."

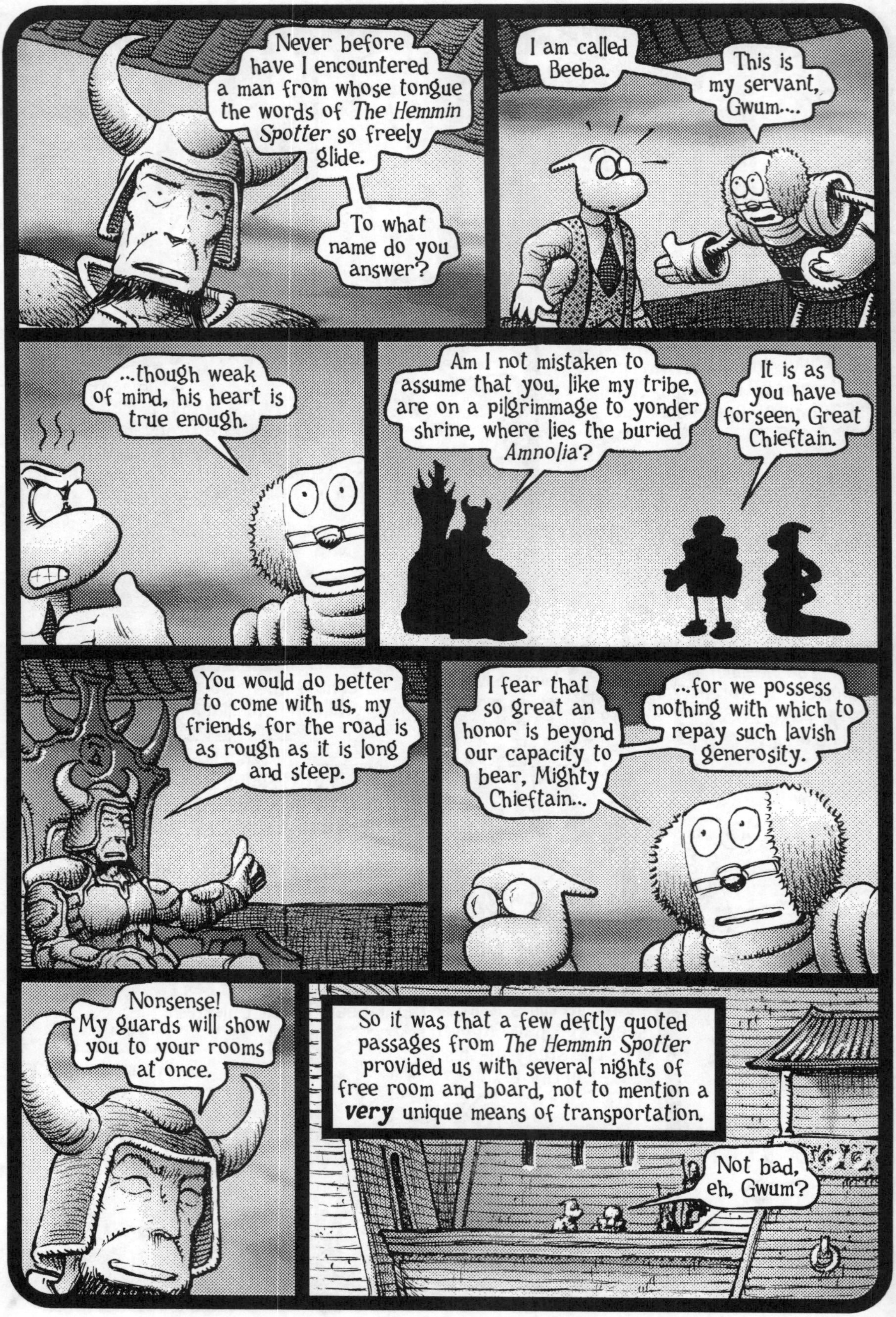
Never before have I encountered a man from whose tongue the words of *The Hemmin Spotter* so freely glide.
To what name do you answer?
I am called Beeba.
This is my servant, Gwum....
...though weak of mind, his heart is true enough.
Am I not mistaken to assume that you, like my tribe, are on a pilgrimmage to yonder shrine, where lies the buried *Amnolia*?
It is as you have forseen, Great Chieftain.
You would do better to come with us, my friends, for the road is as rough as it is long and steep.
I fear that so great an honor is beyond our capacity to bear, Mighty Chieftain...
...for we possess nothing with which to repay such lavish generosity.
Nonsense! My guards will show you to your rooms at once.
So it was that a few deftly quoted passages from *The Hemmin Spotter* provided us with several nights of free room and board, not to mention a ***very*** unique means of transportation.
Not bad, eh, Gwum?

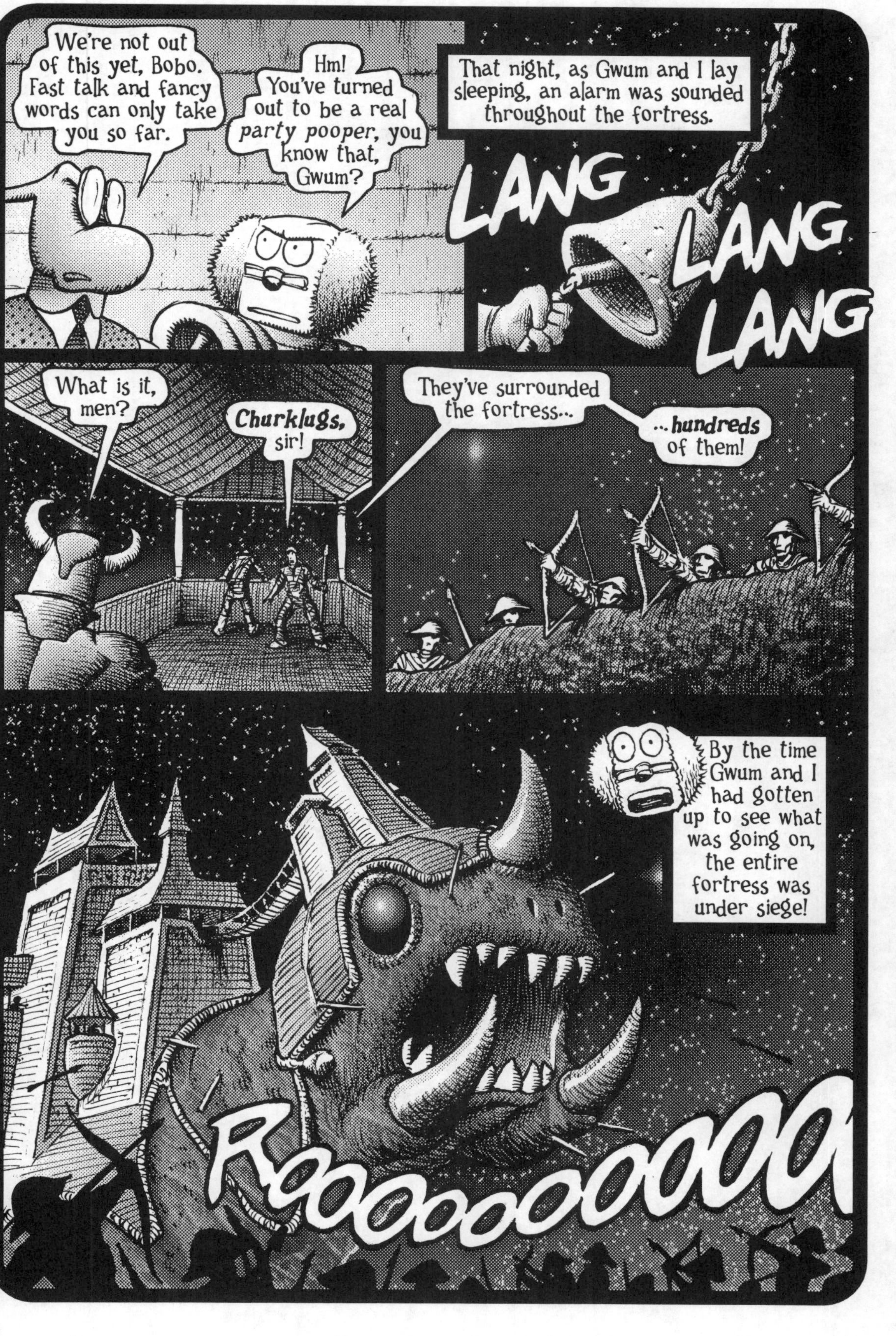

We're not out of this yet, Bobo. Fast talk and fancy words can only take you so far.
Hm! You've turned out to be a real *party pooper*, you know that, Gwum?
That night, as Gwum and I lay sleeping, an alarm was sounded throughout the fortress.
LANG
LANG
LANG
What is it, men?
Churklugs, sir!
They've surrounded the fortress...
...**hundreds** of them!
By the time Gwum and I had gotten up to see what was going on, the entire fortress was under siege!
Raooooooooo

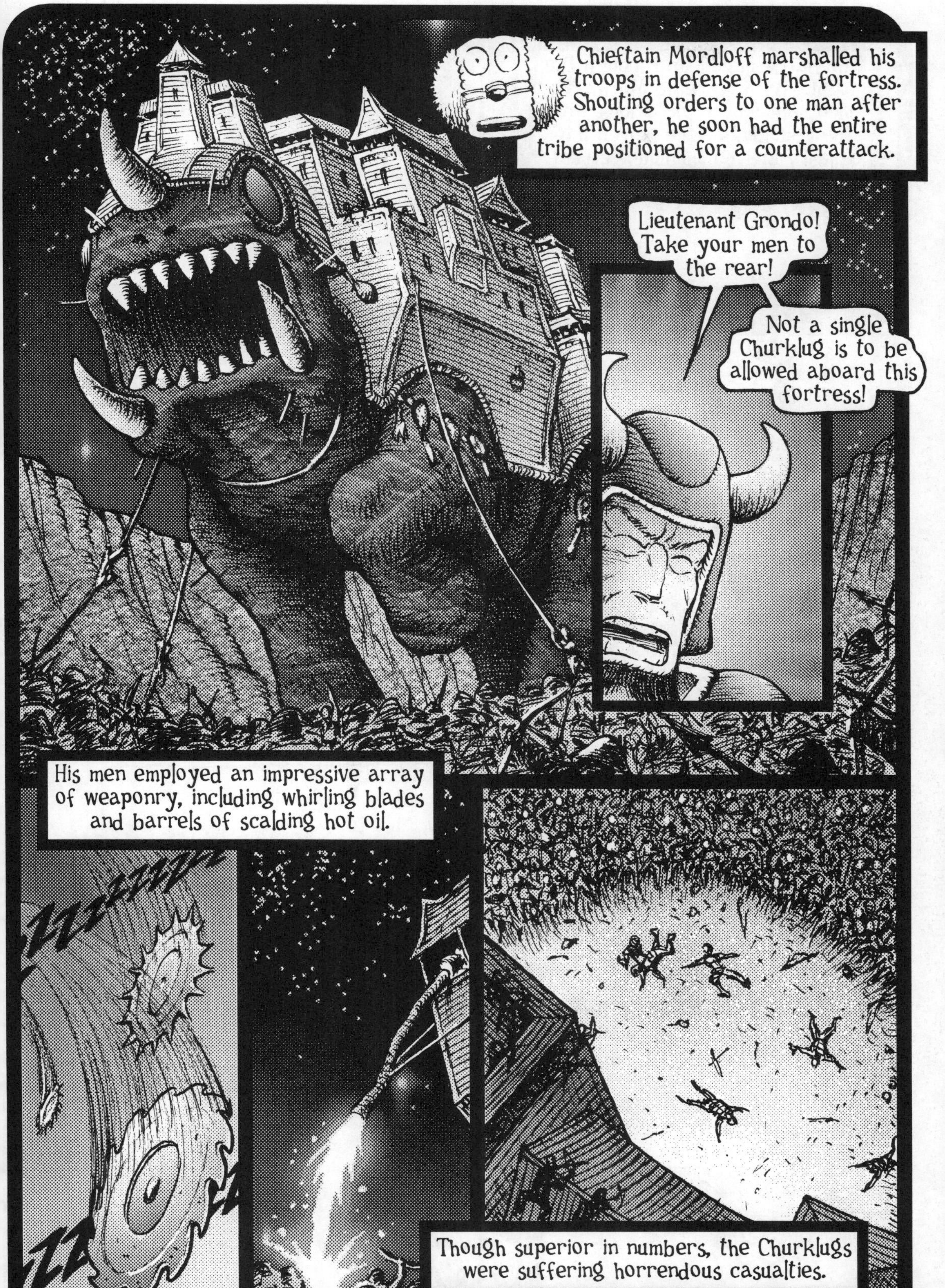
Chieftain Mordloff marshalled his troops in defense of the fortress. Shouting orders to one man after another, he soon had the entire tribe positioned for a counterattack.
Lieutenant Grondo! Take your men to the rear!
Not a single Churklug is to be allowed aboard this fortress!
His men employed an impressive array of weaponry, including whirling blades and barrels of scalding hot oil.
Though superior in numbers, the Churklugs were suffering horrendous casualties.

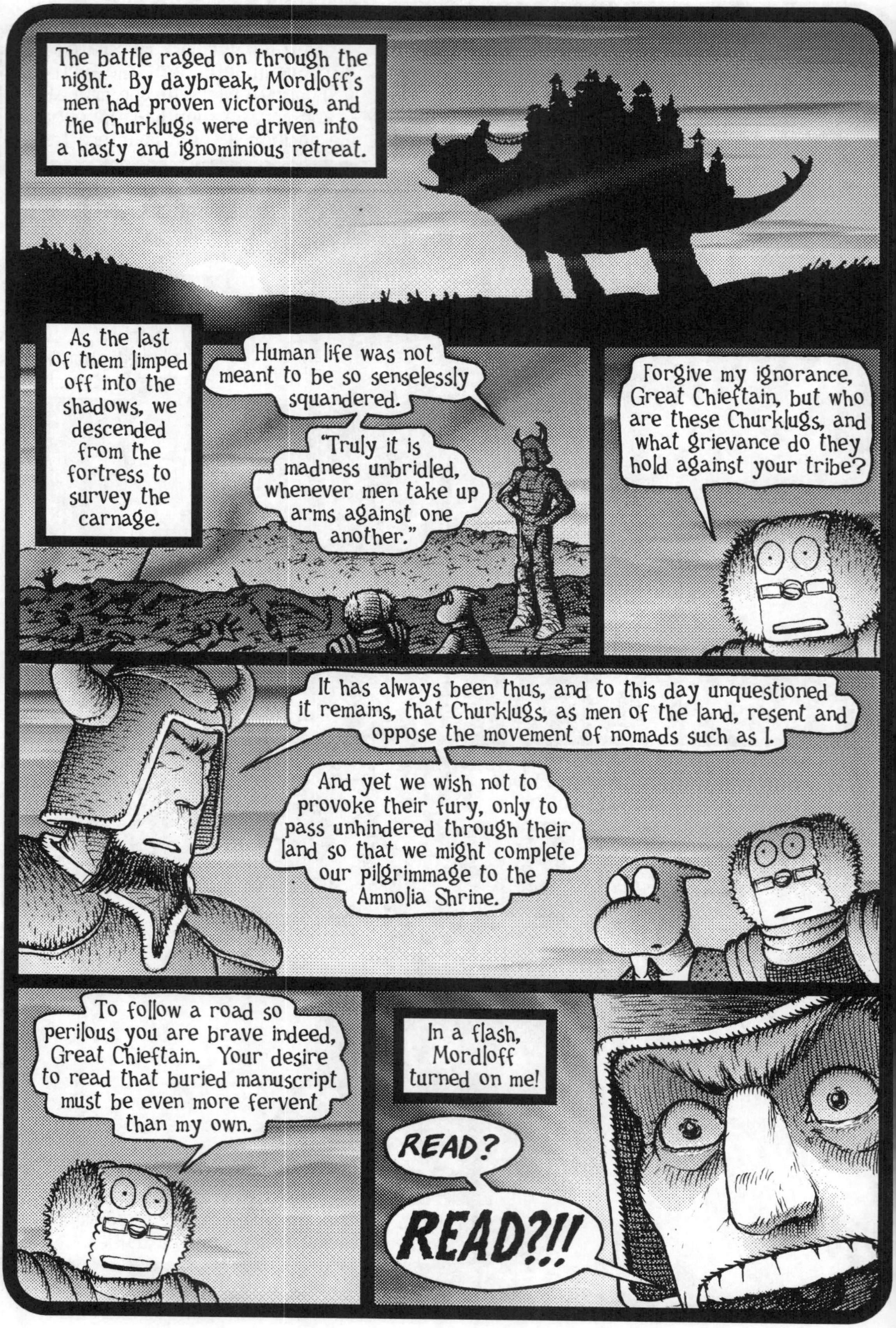

The battle raged on through the night. By daybreak, Mordloff's men had proven victorious, and the Churklugs were driven into a hasty and ignominious retreat.
As the last of them limped off into the shadows, we descended from the fortress to survey the carnage.
Human life was not meant to be so senselessly squandered.
"Truly it is madness unbridled, whenever men take up arms against one another."
Forgive my ignorance, Great Chieftain, but who are these Churklugs, and what grievance do they hold against your tribe?
It has always been thus, and to this day unquestioned it remains, that Churklugs, as men of the land, resent and oppose the movement of nomads such as I.
And yet we wish not to provoke their fury, only to pass unhindered through their land so that we might complete our pilgrimmage to the Amnolia Shrine.
To follow a road so perilous you are brave indeed, Great Chieftain. Your desire to read that buried manuscript must be even more fervent than my own.
In a flash, Mordloff turned on me!
READ?
READ?!!

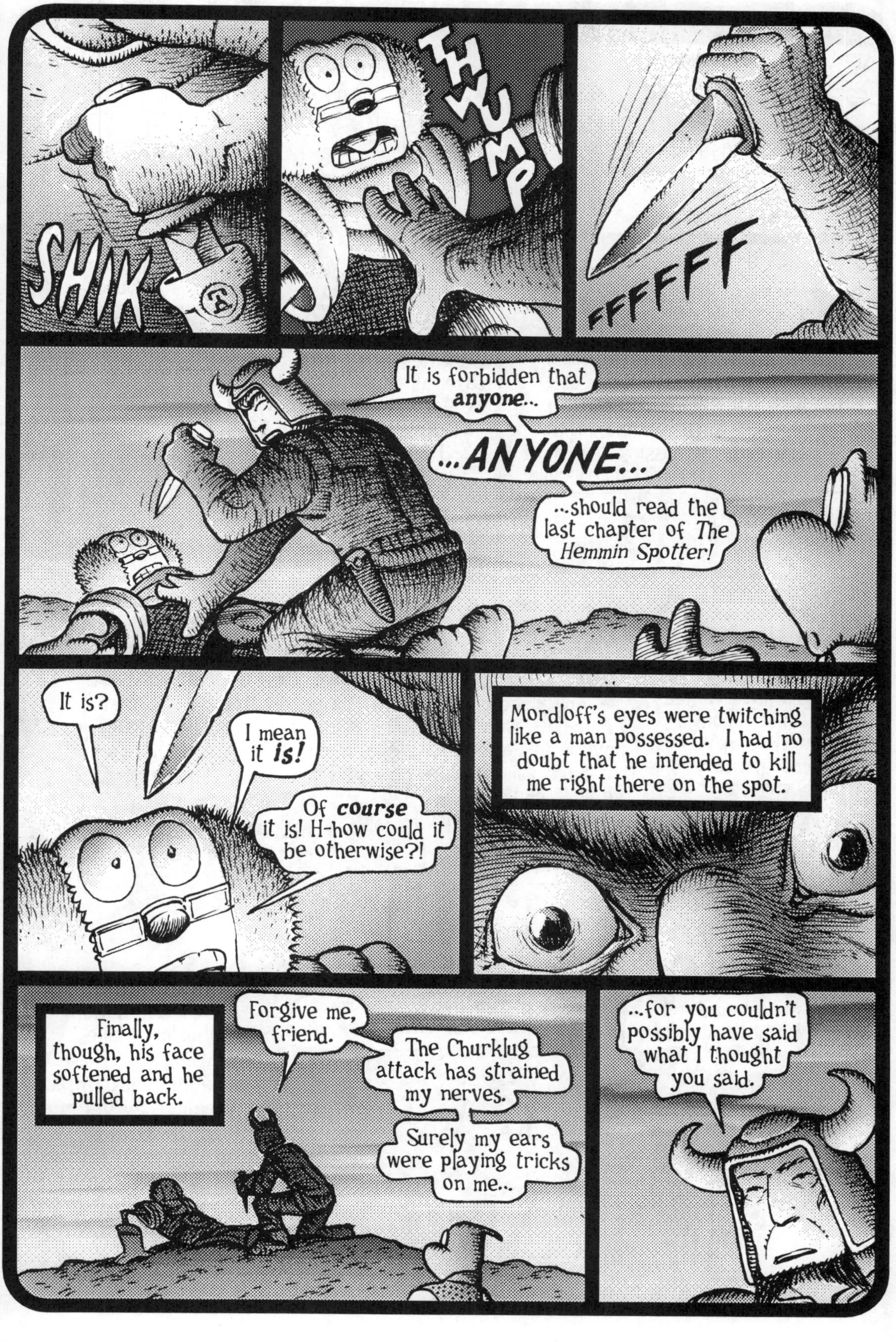
SHIK
THWUMP
FFFFFFF
It is forbidden that **anyone**...
...ANYONE...
...should read the last chapter of *The Hemmin Spotter!*
It is?
I mean it **is!**
Of **course** it is! H-how could it be otherwise?!
Mordloff's eyes were twitching like a man possessed. I had no doubt that he intended to kill me right there on the spot.
Finally, though, his face softened and he pulled back.
Forgive me, friend.
The Churklug attack has strained my nerves.
Surely my ears were playing tricks on me...
...for you couldn't possibly have said what I thought you said.

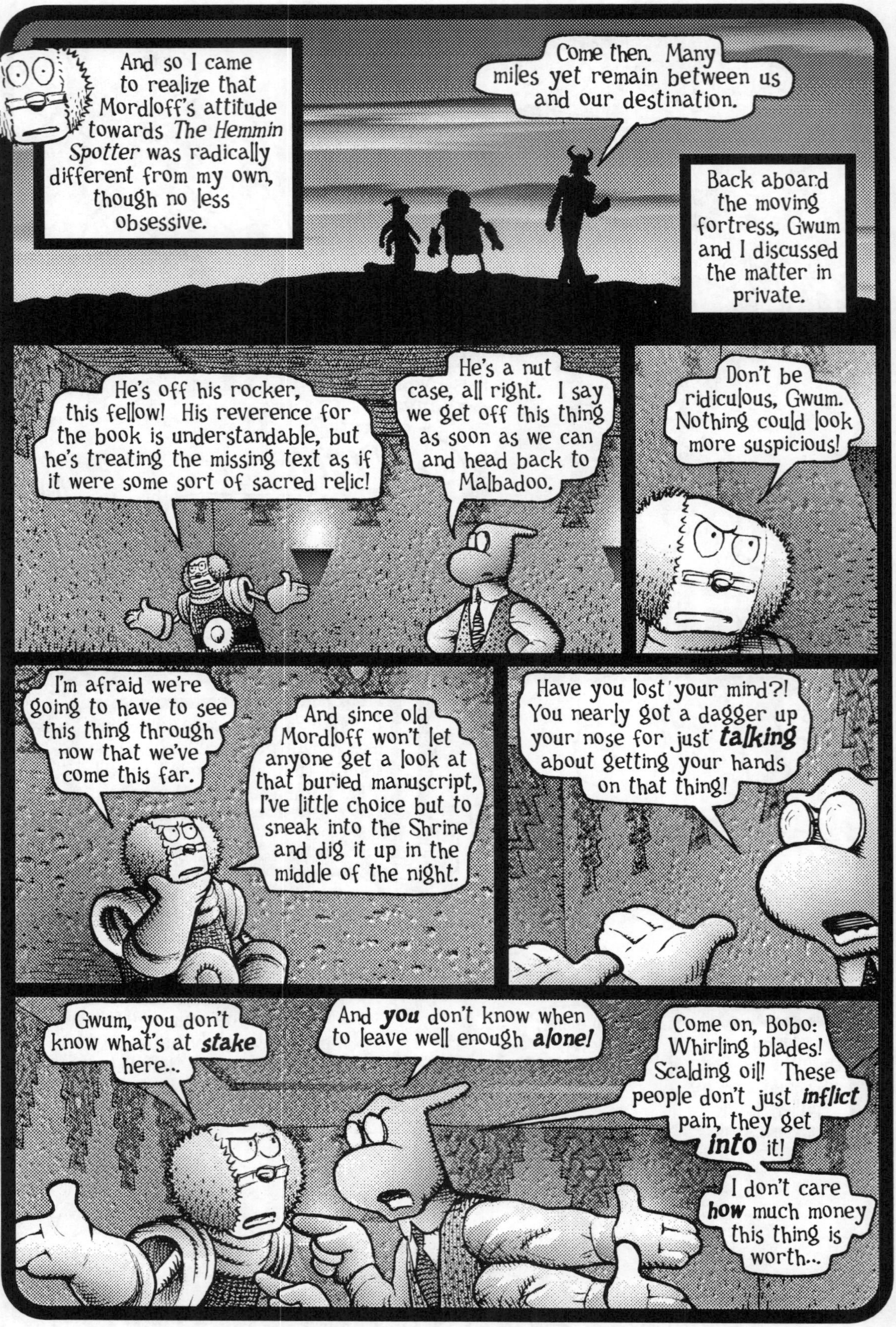
And so I came to realize that Mordloff's attitude towards *The Hemmin Spotter* was radically different from my own, though no less obsessive.
Come then. Many miles yet remain between us and our destination.
Back aboard the moving fortress, Gwum and I discussed the matter in private.
He's off his rocker, this fellow! His reverence for the book is understandable, but he's treating the missing text as if it were some sort of sacred relic!
He's a nut case, all right. I say we get off this thing as soon as we can and head back to Malbadoo.
Don't be ridiculous, Gwum. Nothing could look more suspicious!
I'm afraid we're going to have to see this thing through now that we've come this far.
And since old Mordloff won't let anyone get a look at that buried manuscript, I've little choice but to sneak into the Shrine and dig it up in the middle of the night.
Have you lost your mind?! You nearly got a dagger up your nose for just ***talking*** about getting your hands on that thing!
Gwum, you don't know what's at ***stake*** here...
And ***you*** don't know when to leave well enough ***alone!***
Come on, Bobo: Whirling blades! Scalding oil! These people don't just ***inflict*** pain, they get ***into*** it!
I don't care ***how*** much money this thing is worth...

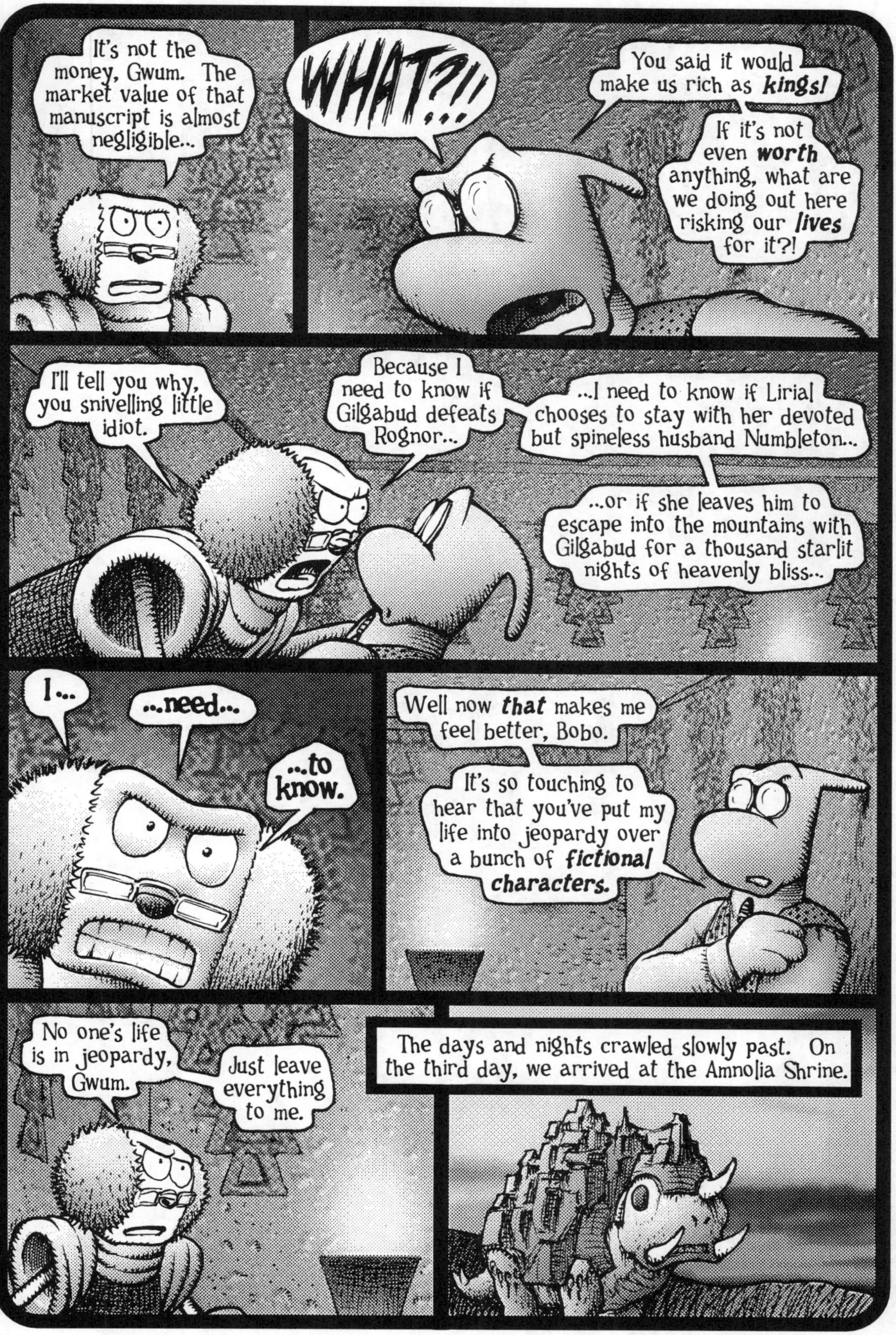

It's not the money, Gwum. The market value of that manuscript is almost negligible...
WHAT?!...
You said it would make us rich as kings!
If it's not even worth anything, what are we doing out here risking our lives for it?!
I'll tell you why, you snivelling little idiot.
Because I need to know if Gilgabud defeats Rognor...
...I need to know if Lirial chooses to stay with her devoted but spineless husband Numbleton...
...or if she leaves him to escape into the mountains with Gilgabud for a thousand starlit nights of heavenly bliss...
I...
...need...
...to know.
Well now that makes me feel better, Bobo.
It's so touching to hear that you've put my life into jeopardy over a bunch of fictional characters.
No one's life is in jeopardy, Gwum.
Just leave everything to me.
The days and nights crawled slowly past. On the third day, we arrived at the Amnolia Shrine.

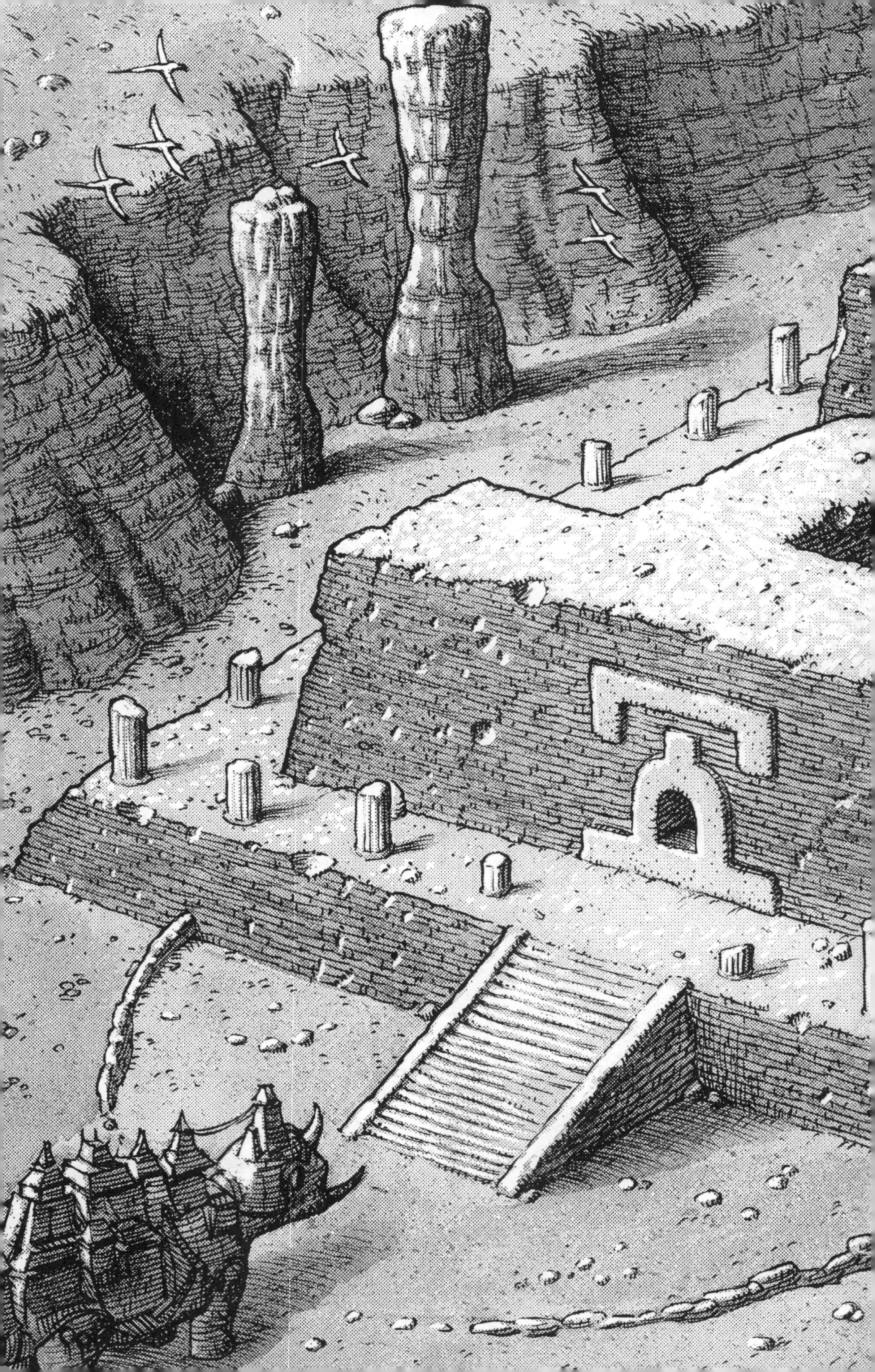

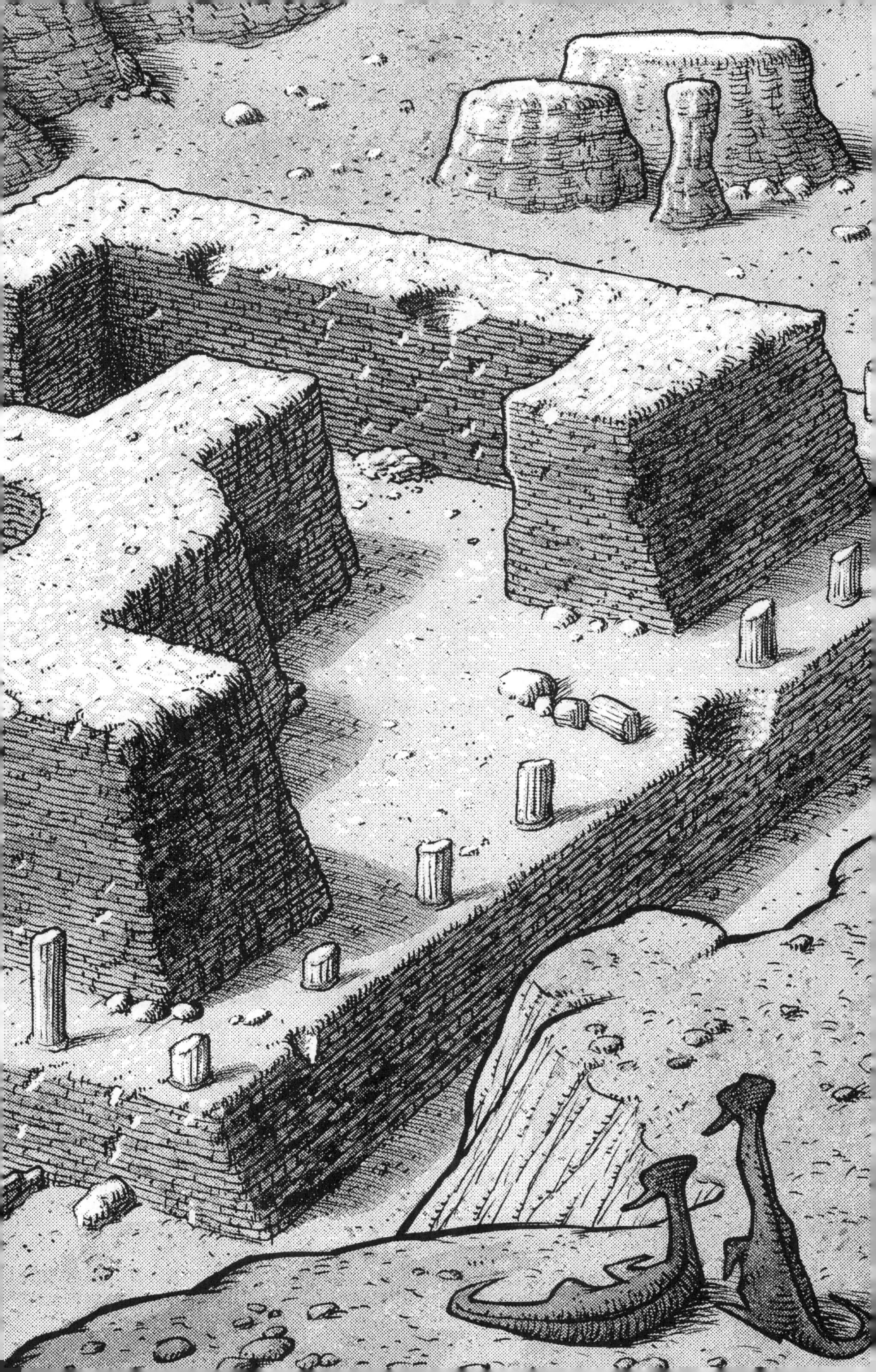

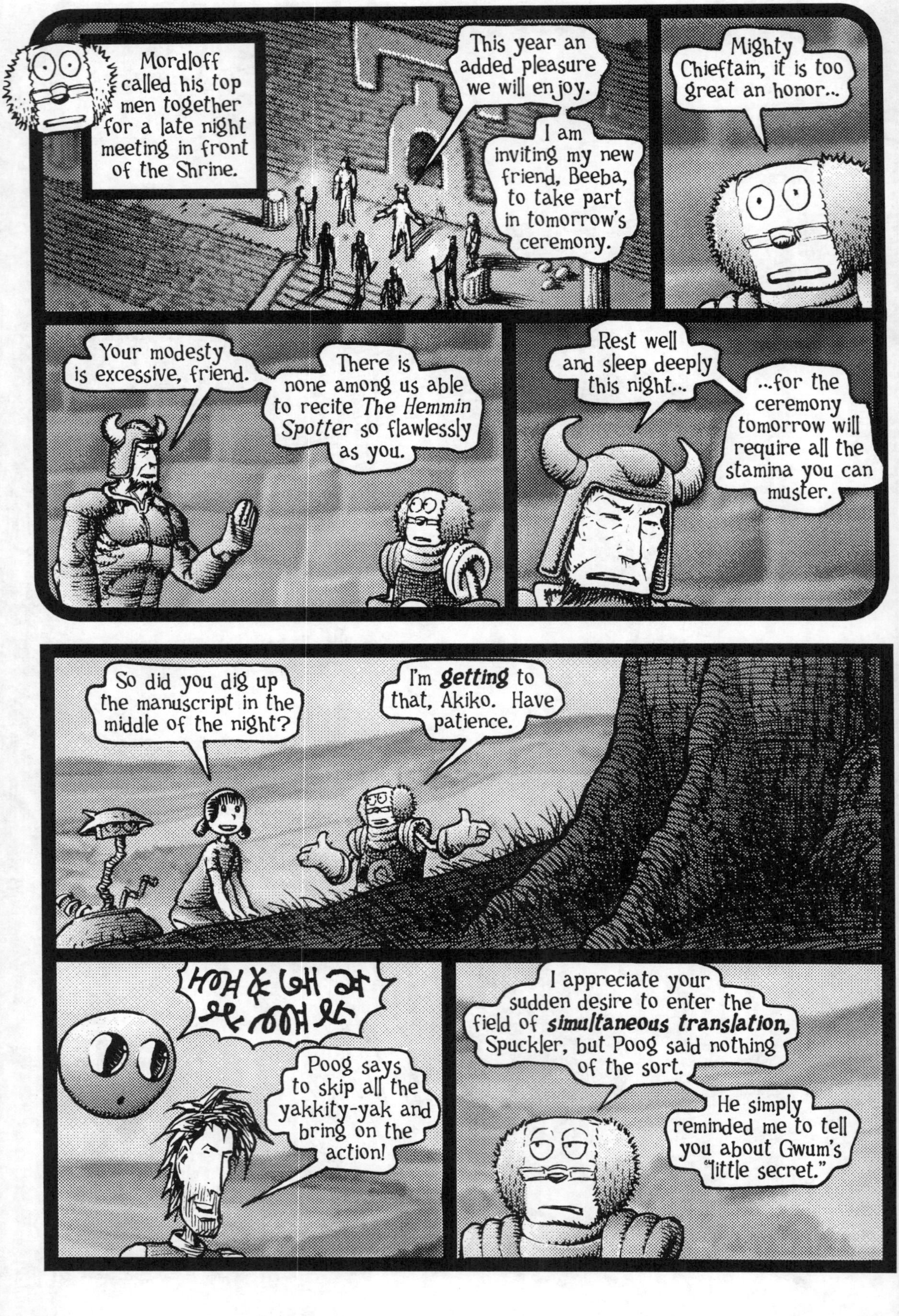
Mordloff called his top men together for a late night meeting in front of the Shrine.
This year an added pleasure we will enjoy.
I am inviting my new friend, Beeba, to take part in tomorrow's ceremony.
Mighty Chieftain, it is too great an honor...
Your modesty is excessive, friend.
There is none among us able to recite *The Hemmin Spotter* so flawlessly as you.
Rest well and sleep deeply this night...
...for the ceremony tomorrow will require all the stamina you can muster.
So did you dig up the manuscript in the middle of the night?
I'm ***getting*** to that, Akiko. Have patience.
Poog says to skip all the yakkity-yak and bring on the action!
I appreciate your sudden desire to enter the field of ***simultaneous translation,*** Spuckler, but Poog said nothing of the sort.
He simply reminded me to tell you about Gwum's "little secret."

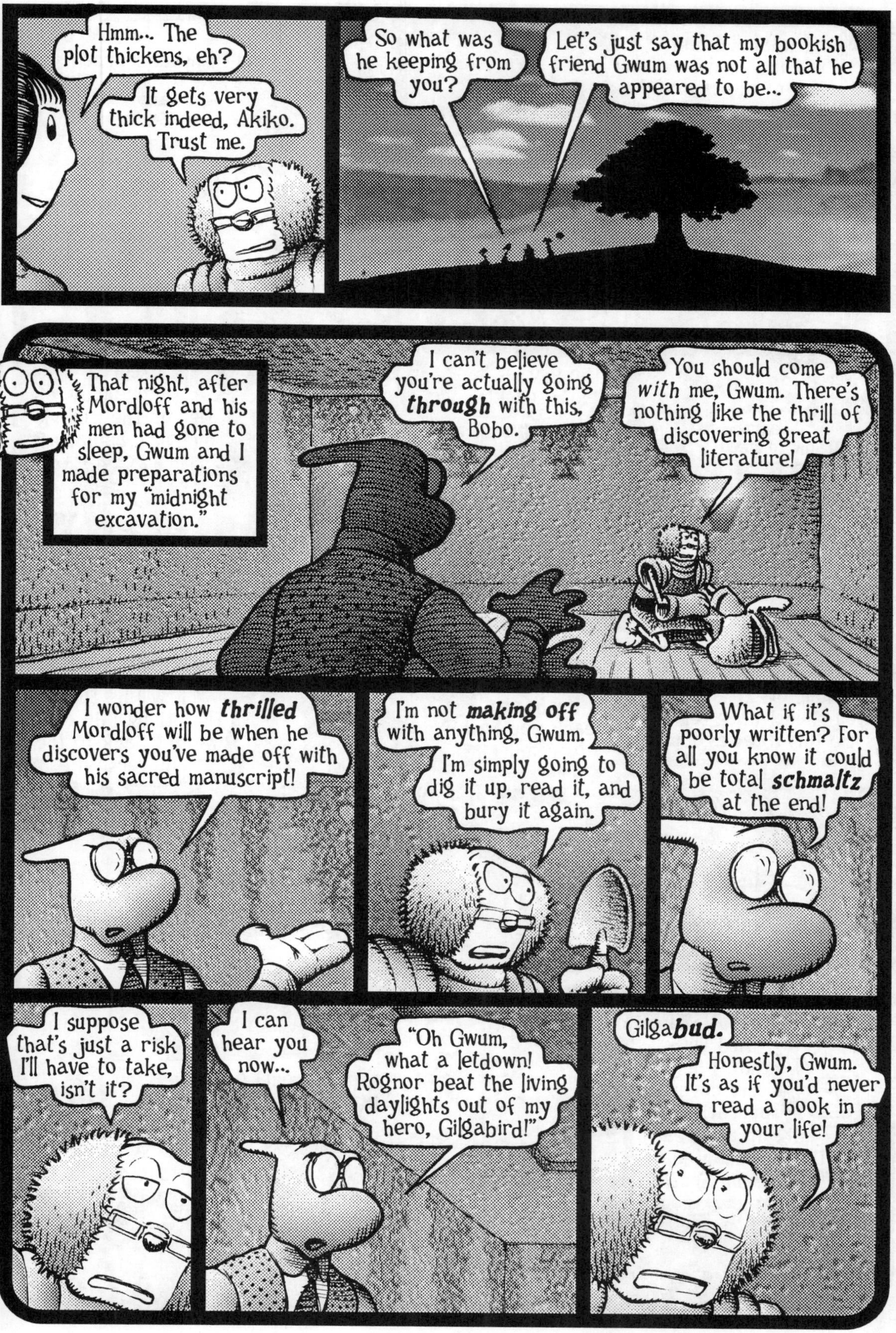
Hmm... The plot thickens, eh?
It gets very thick indeed, Akiko. Trust me.
So what was he keeping from you?
Let's just say that my bookish friend Gwum was not all that he appeared to be...
That night, after Mordloff and his men had gone to sleep, Gwum and I made preparations for my "midnight excavation."
I can't believe you're actually going **through** with this, Bobo.
You should come *with* me, Gwum. There's nothing like the thrill of discovering great literature!
I wonder how **thrilled** Mordloff will be when he discovers you've made off with his sacred manuscript!
I'm not **making off** with anything, Gwum.
I'm simply going to dig it up, read it, and bury it again.
What if it's poorly written? For all you know it could be total **schmaltz** at the end!
I suppose that's just a risk I'll have to take, isn't it?
I can hear you now...
"Oh Gwum, what a letdown! Rognor beat the living daylights out of my hero, Gilgabird!"
Gilga**bud.**
Honestly, Gwum. It's as if you'd never read a book in your life!

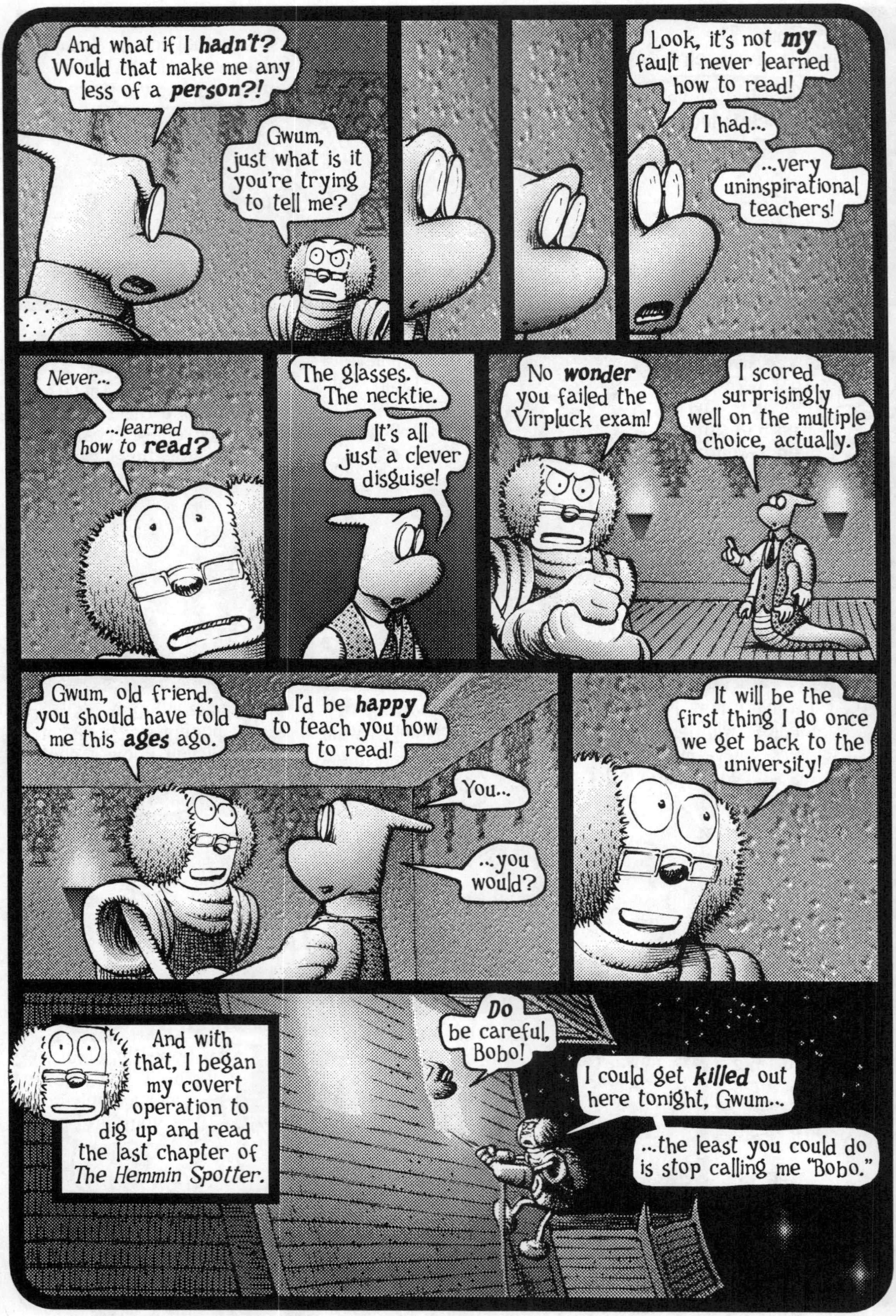
And what if I hadn't? Would that make me any less of a person?!
Gwum, just what is it you're trying to tell me?
Look, it's not my fault I never learned how to read!
I had...
...very uninspirational teachers!
Never...
...learned how to read?
The glasses. The necktie.
It's all just a clever disguise!
No wonder you failed the Virpluck exam!
I scored surprisingly well on the multiple choice, actually.
Gwum, old friend, you should have told me this ages ago.
I'd be happy to teach you how to read!
You...
...you would?
It will be the first thing I do once we get back to the university!
And with that, I began my covert operation to dig up and read the last chapter of The Hemmin Spotter.
Do be careful, Bobo!
I could get killed out here tonight, Gwum...
...the least you could do is stop calling me "Bobo."

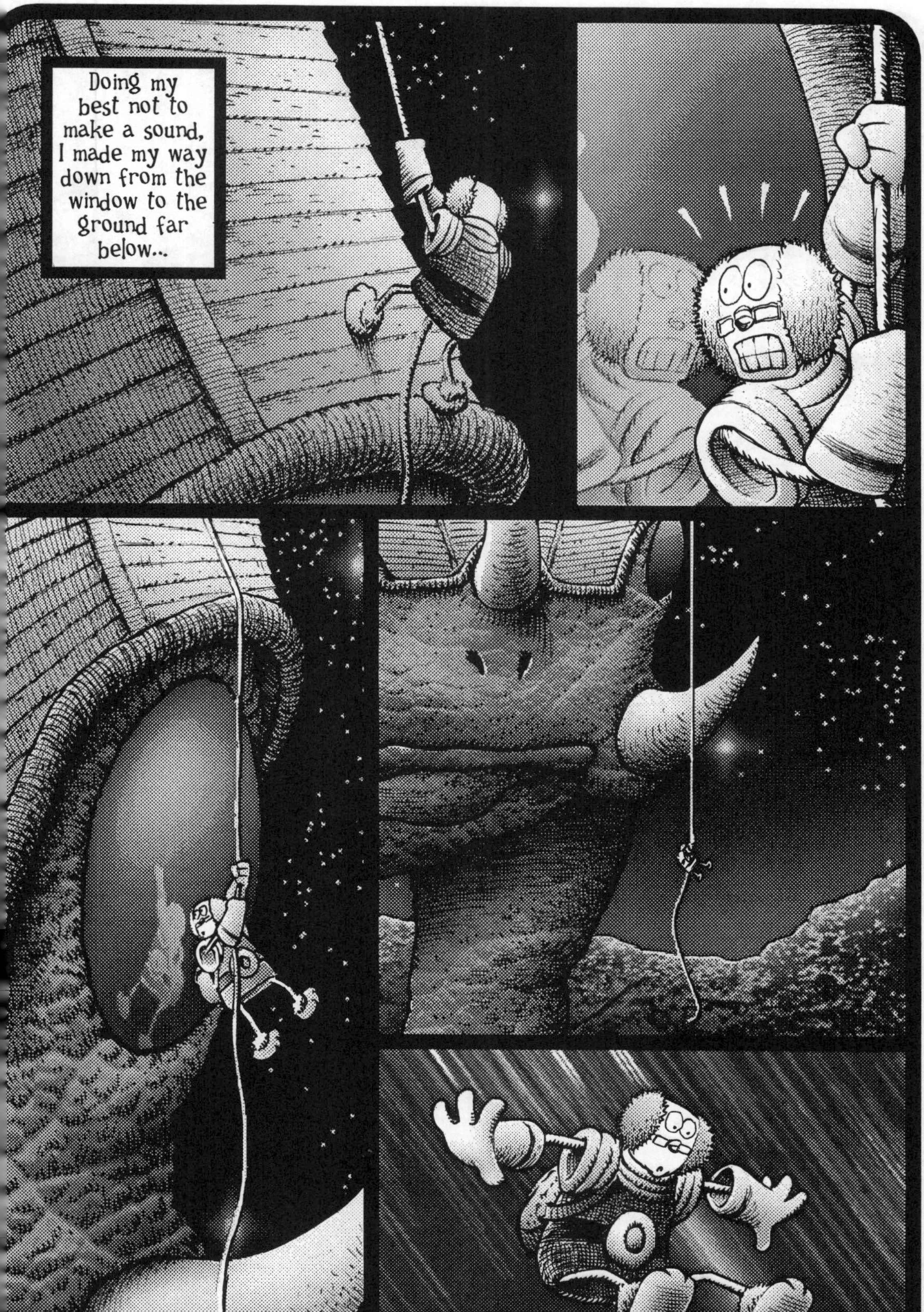
Doing my best not to make a sound, I made my way down from the window to the ground far below...

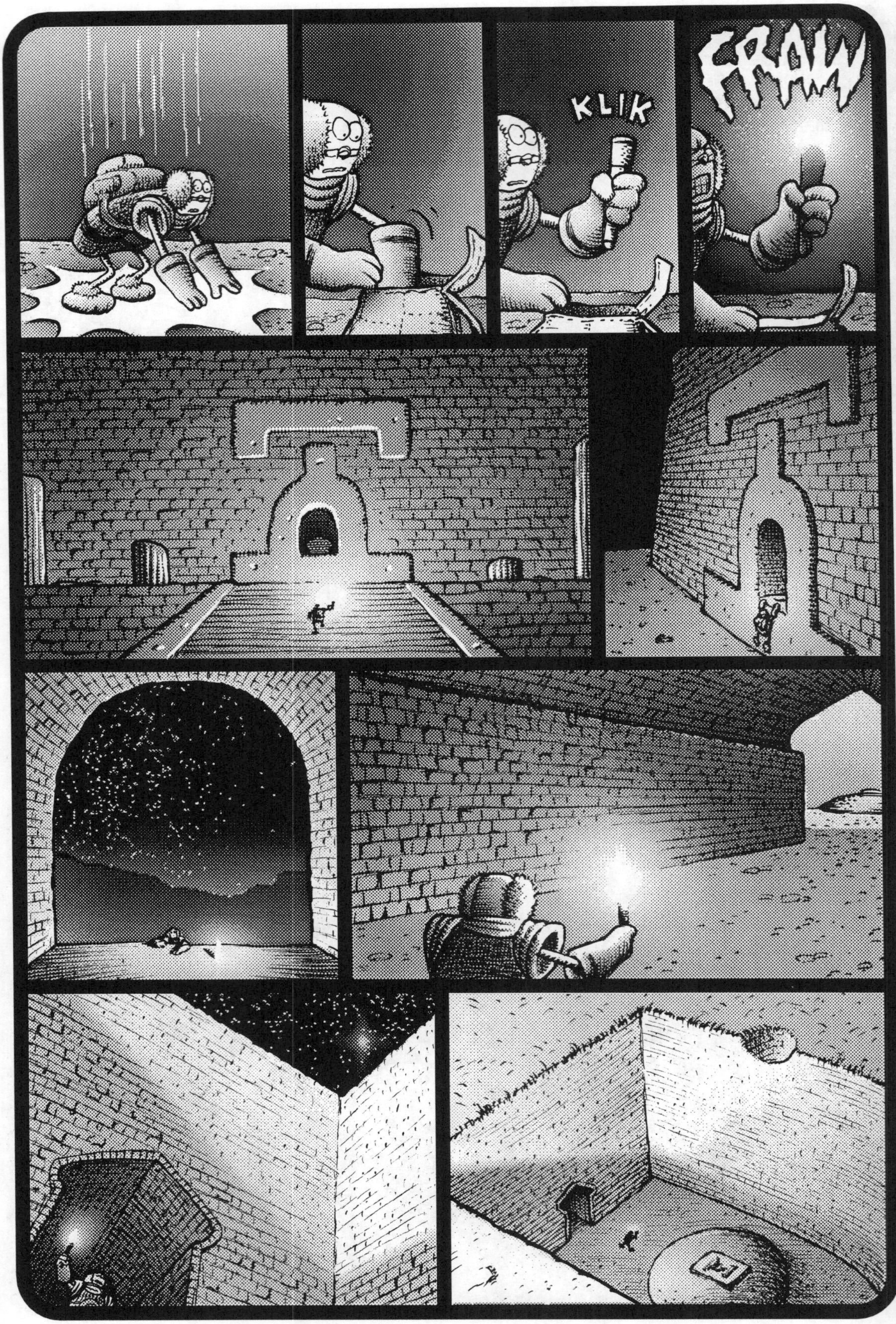
KLIK
FRAW

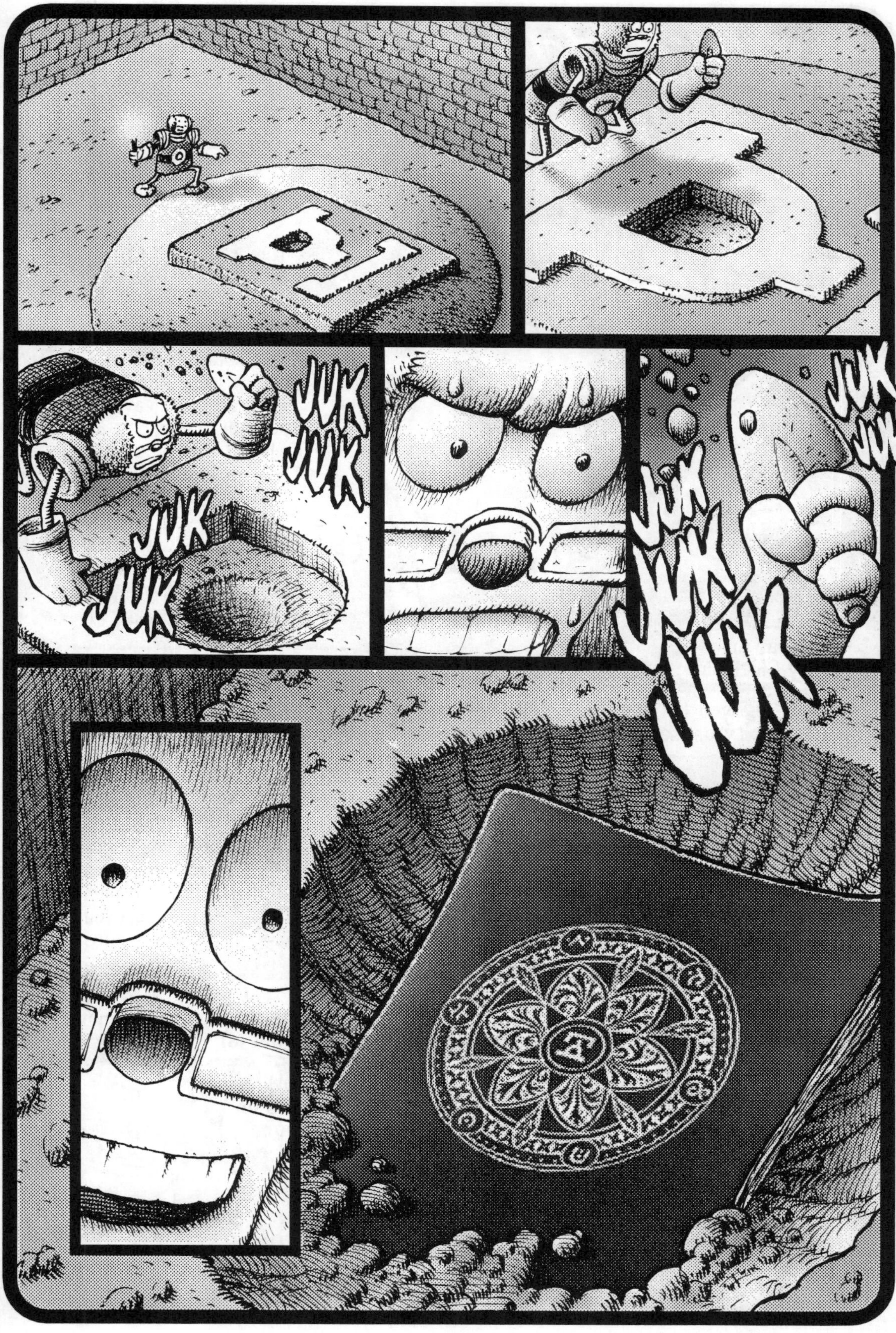
JUK
JUK
JUK
JUK
JUK
JUK
JUK
JUK
JUK
JUK

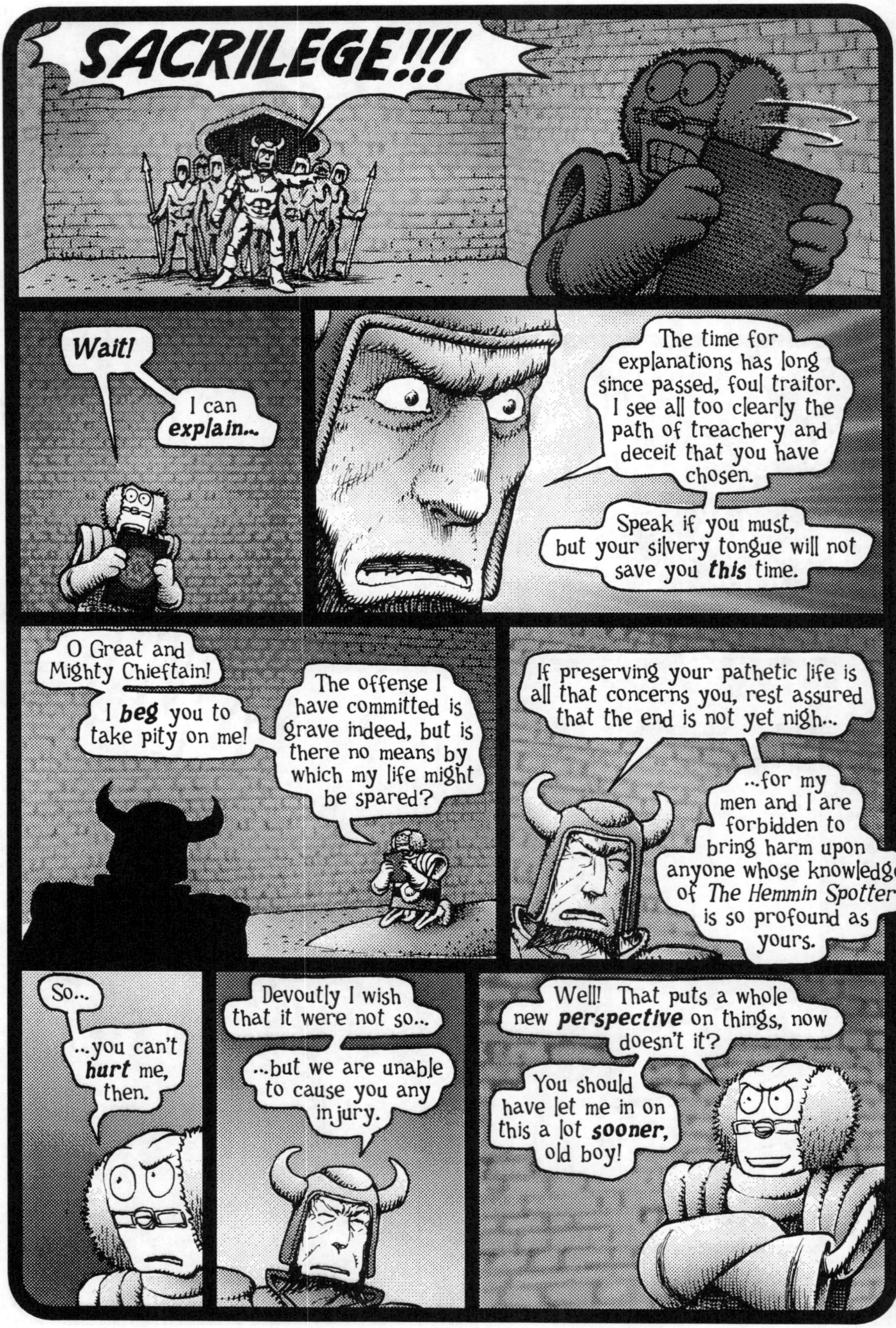
SACRILEGE!!!
Wait!
I can *explain...*
The time for explanations has long since passed, foul traitor. I see all too clearly the path of treachery and deceit that you have chosen.
Speak if you must, but your silvery tongue will not save you *this* time.
O Great and Mighty Chieftain!
I *beg* you to take pity on me!
The offense I have committed is grave indeed, but is there no means by which my life might be spared?
If preserving your pathetic life is all that concerns you, rest assured that the end is not yet nigh...
...for my men and I are forbidden to bring harm upon anyone whose knowledge of *The Hemmin Spotter* is so profound as yours.
So...
...you can't *hurt* me, then.
Devoutly I wish that it were not so...
...but we are unable to cause you any injury.
Well! That puts a whole new *perspective* on things, now doesn't it?
You should have let me in on this a lot *sooner*, old boy!

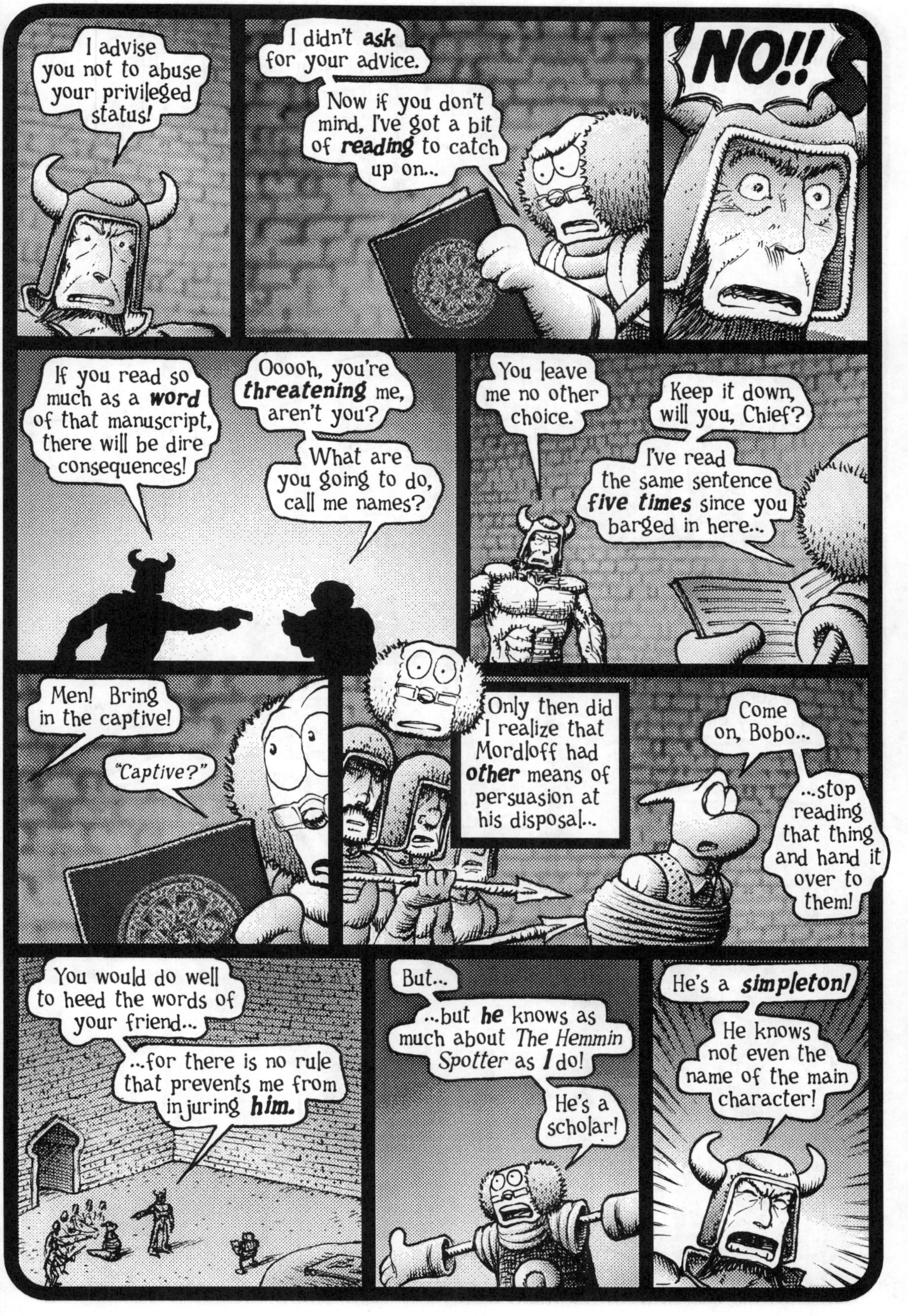

I advise you not to abuse your privileged status!
I didn't ask for your advice.
Now if you don't mind, I've got a bit of reading to catch up on...
NO!!
If you read so much as a word of that manuscript, there will be dire consequences!
Ooooh, you're threatening me, aren't you?
What are you going to do, call me names?
You leave me no other choice.
Keep it down, will you, Chief?
I've read the same sentence five times since you barged in here...
Men! Bring in the captive!
"Captive?"
Only then did I realize that Mordloff had other means of persuasion at his disposal...
Come on, Bobo...
...stop reading that thing and hand it over to them!
You would do well to heed the words of your friend...
...for there is no rule that prevents me from injuring him.
But...
...but he knows as much about The Hemmin Spotter as I do!
He's a scholar!
He's a simpleton!
He knows not even the name of the main character!

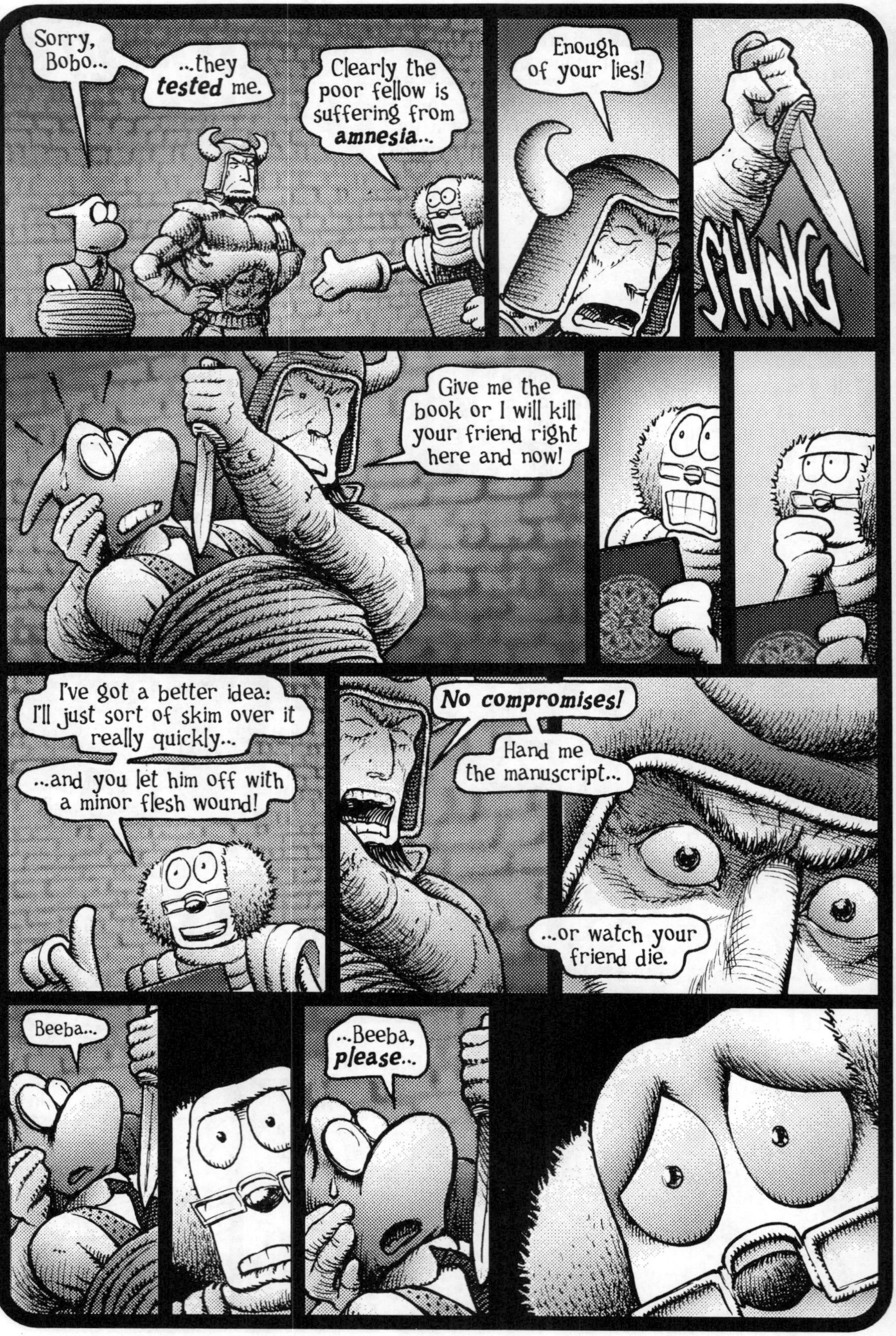

Sorry, Bobo...
...they tested me.
Clearly the poor fellow is suffering from amnesia...
Enough of your lies!
SHING
Give me the book or I will kill your friend right here and now!
I've got a better idea: I'll just sort of skim over it really quickly...
...and you let him off with a minor flesh wound!
No compromises!
Hand me the manuscript...
...or watch your friend die.
Beeba...
...Beeba, please...

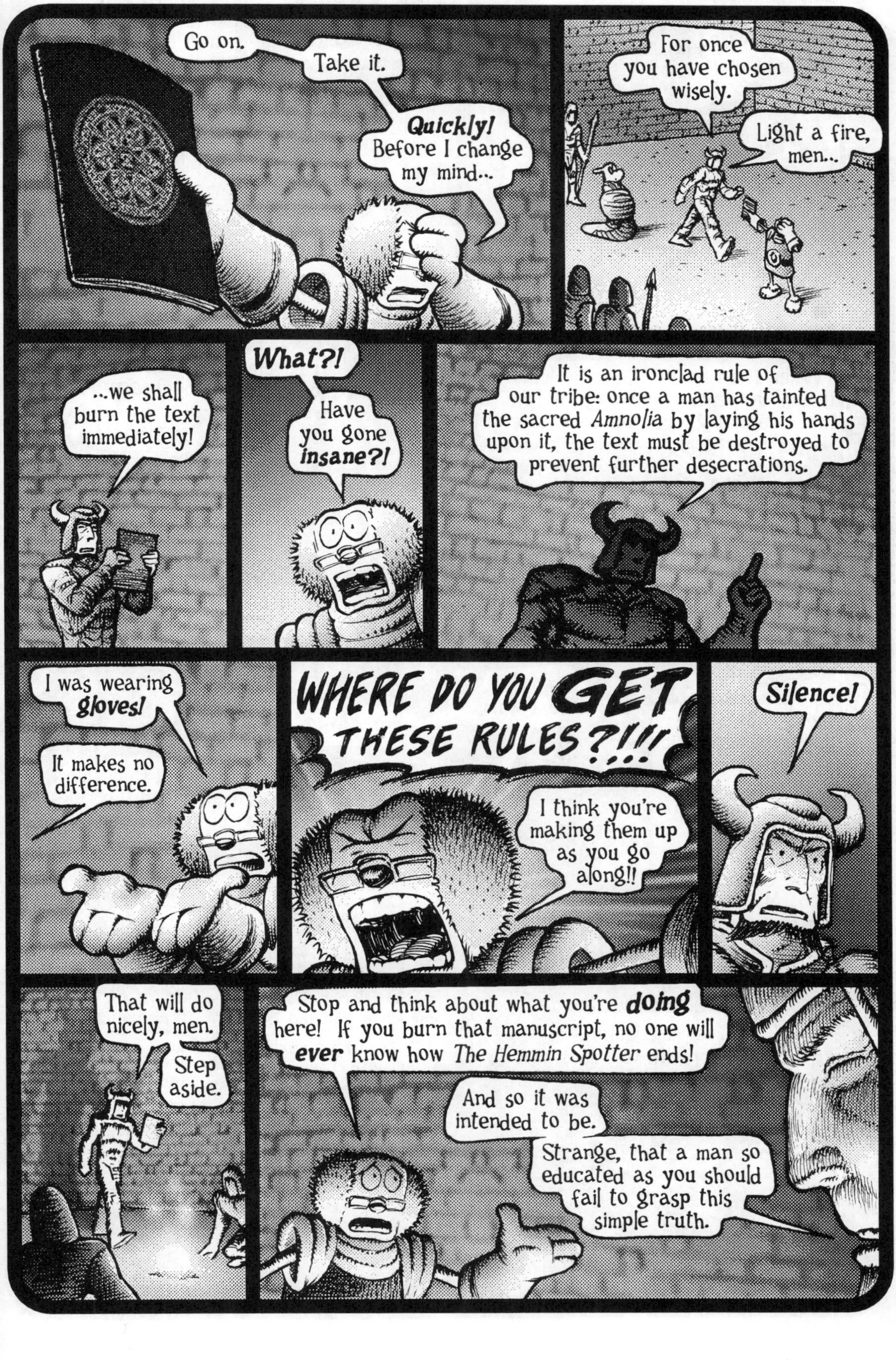
Go on.
Take it.
Quickly! Before I change my mind...
For once you have chosen wisely.
Light a fire, men...
...we shall burn the text immediately!
What?!
Have you gone insane?!
It is an ironclad rule of our tribe: once a man has tainted the sacred Amnolia by laying his hands upon it, the text must be destroyed to prevent further desecrations.
I was wearing gloves!
It makes no difference.
WHERE DO YOU GET THESE RULES?!!!
I think you're making them up as you go along!!
Silence!
That will do nicely, men.
Step aside.
Stop and think about what you're doing here! If you burn that manuscript, no one will ever know how The Hemmin Spotter ends!
And so it was intended to be.
Strange, that a man so educated as you should fail to grasp this simple truth.

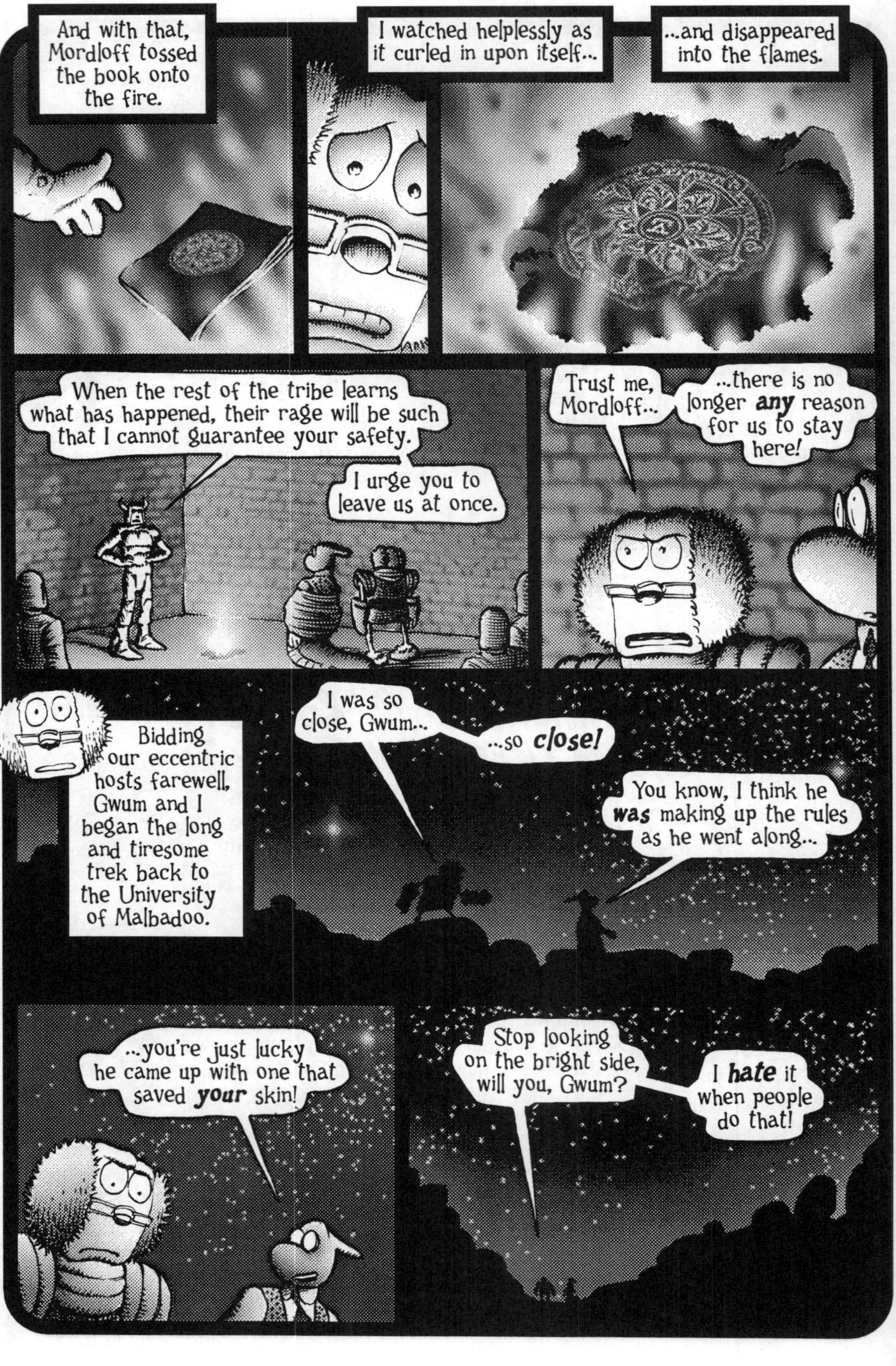

And with that, Mordloff tossed the book onto the fire.
I watched helplessly as it curled in upon itself...
...and disappeared into the flames.
When the rest of the tribe learns what has happened, their rage will be such that I cannot guarantee your safety.
I urge you to leave us at once.
Trust me, Mordloff...
...there is no longer **any** reason for us to stay here!
Bidding our eccentric hosts farewell, Gwum and I began the long and tiresome trek back to the University of Malbadoo.
I was so close, Gwum...
...so ***close!***
You know, I think he **was** making up the rules as he went along...
...you're just lucky he came up with one that saved **your** skin!
Stop looking on the bright side, will you, Gwum?
I ***hate*** it when people do that!

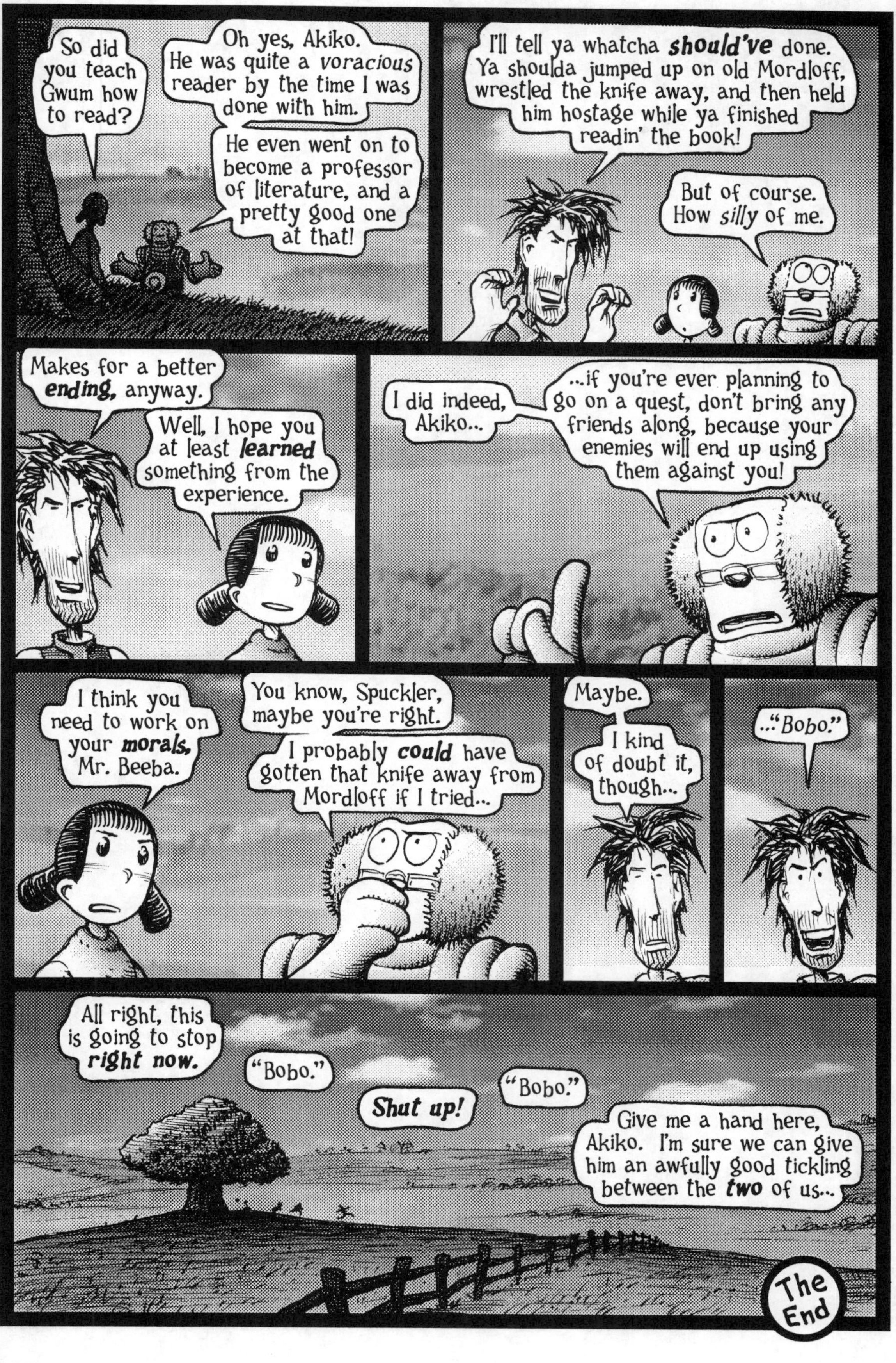
So did you teach Gwum how to read?
Oh yes, Akiko. He was quite a *voracious* reader by the time I was done with him.
He even went on to become a professor of literature, and a pretty good one at that!
I'll tell ya whatcha **should've** done. Ya shoulda jumped up on old Mordloff, wrestled the knife away, and then held him hostage while ya finished readin' the book!
But of course. How *silly* of me.
Makes for a better **ending,** anyway.
Well, I hope you at least **learned** something from the experience.
I did indeed, Akiko...
...if you're ever planning to go on a quest, don't bring any friends along, because your enemies will end up using them against you!
I think you need to work on your **morals,** Mr. Beeba.
You know, Spuckler, maybe you're right.
I probably **could** have gotten that knife away from Mordloff if I tried...
Maybe.
I kind of doubt it, though...
..."Bobo."
All right, this is going to stop **right now.**
"Bobo."
Shut up!
"Bobo."
Give me a hand here, Akiko. I'm sure we can give him an awfully good tickling between the **two** of us...
The End

Spuckler's Tale

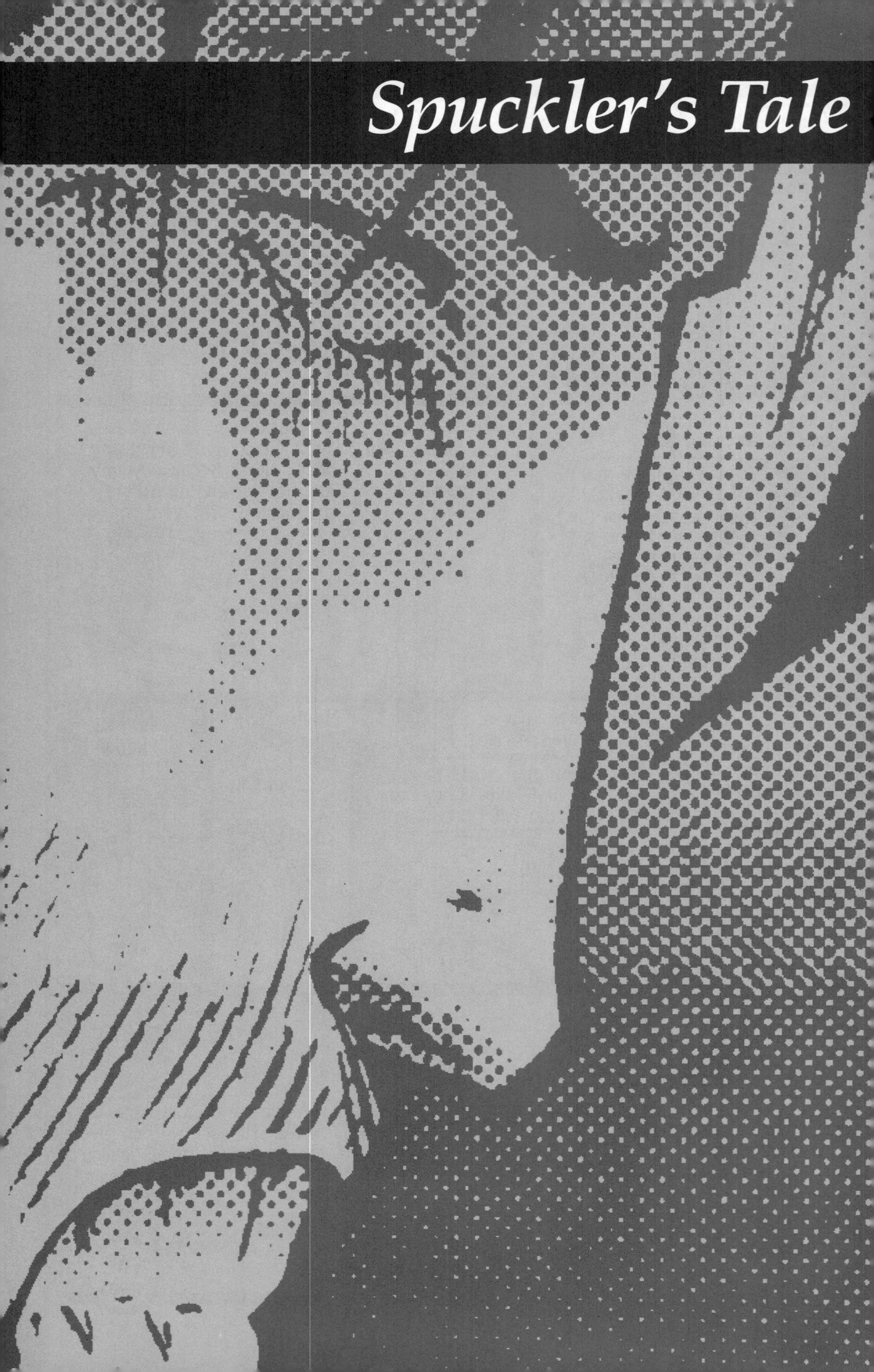

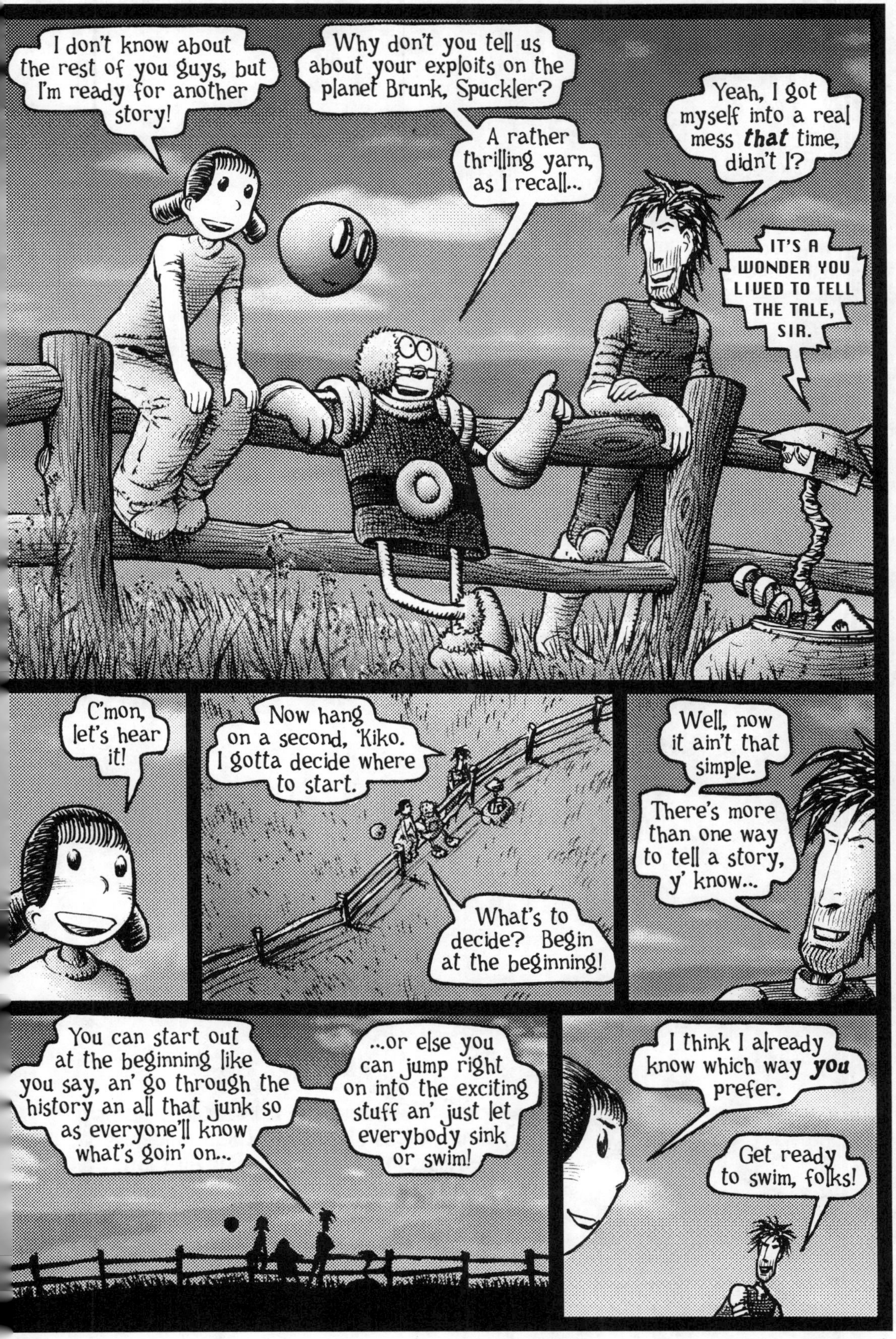
I don't know about the rest of you guys, but I'm ready for another story!
Why don't you tell us about your exploits on the planet Brunk, Spuckler?
A rather thrilling yarn, as I recall...
Yeah, I got myself into a real mess *that* time, didn't I?
IT'S A WONDER YOU LIVED TO TELL THE TALE, SIR.
C'mon, let's hear it!
Now hang on a second, 'Kiko. I gotta decide where to start.
What's to decide? Begin at the beginning!
Well, now it ain't that simple.
There's more than one way to tell a story, y' know...
You can start out at the beginning like you say, an' go through the history an all that junk so as everyone'll know what's goin' on...
...or else you can jump right on into the exciting stuff an' just let everybody sink or swim!
I think I already know which way *you* prefer.
Get ready to swim, folks!

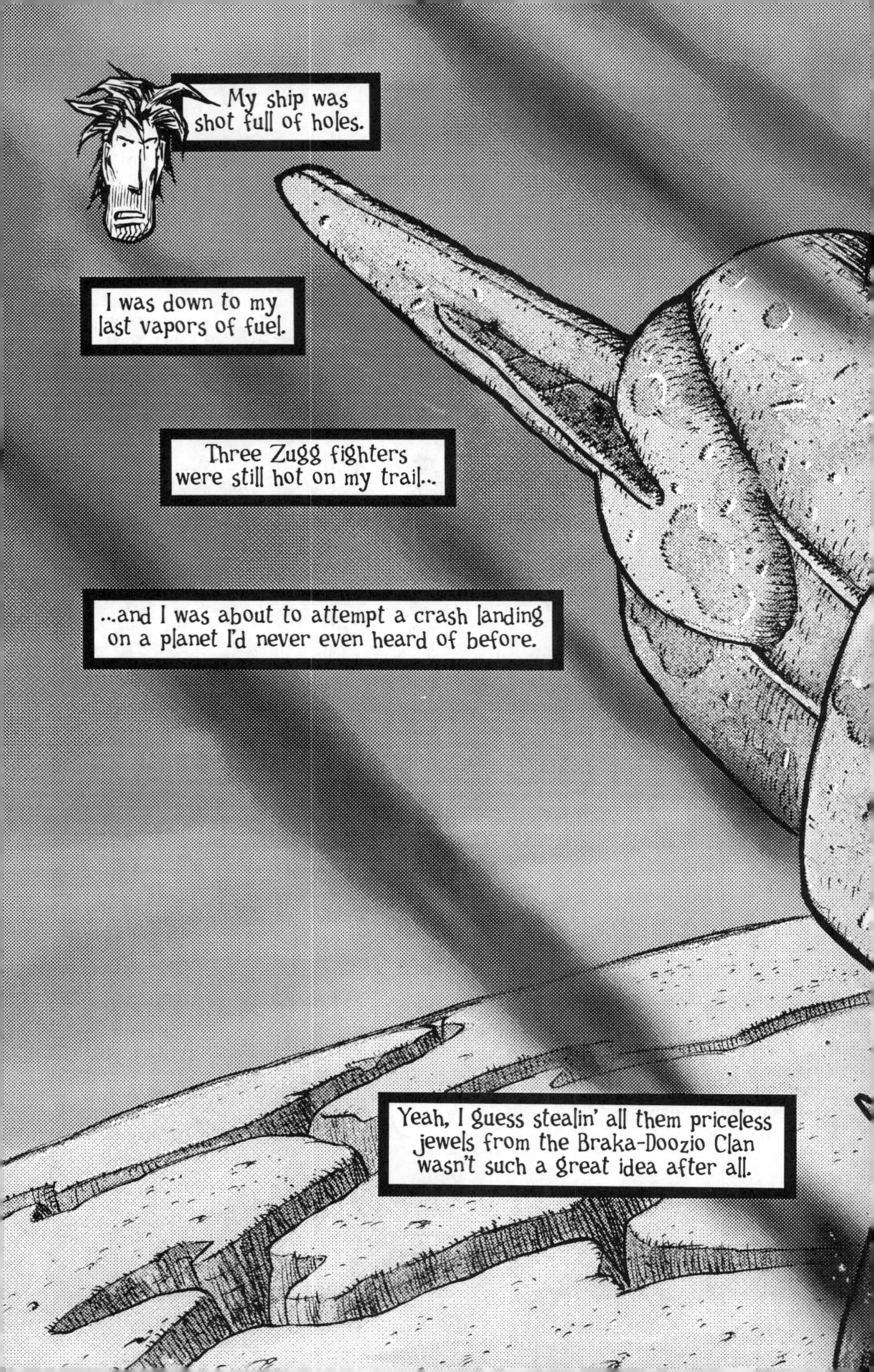
My ship was shot full of holes.
I was down to my last vapors of fuel.
Three Zugg fighters were still hot on my trail...
...and I was about to attempt a crash landing on a planet I'd never even heard of before.
Yeah, I guess stealin' all them priceless jewels from the Braka-Doozio Clan wasn't such a great idea after all.

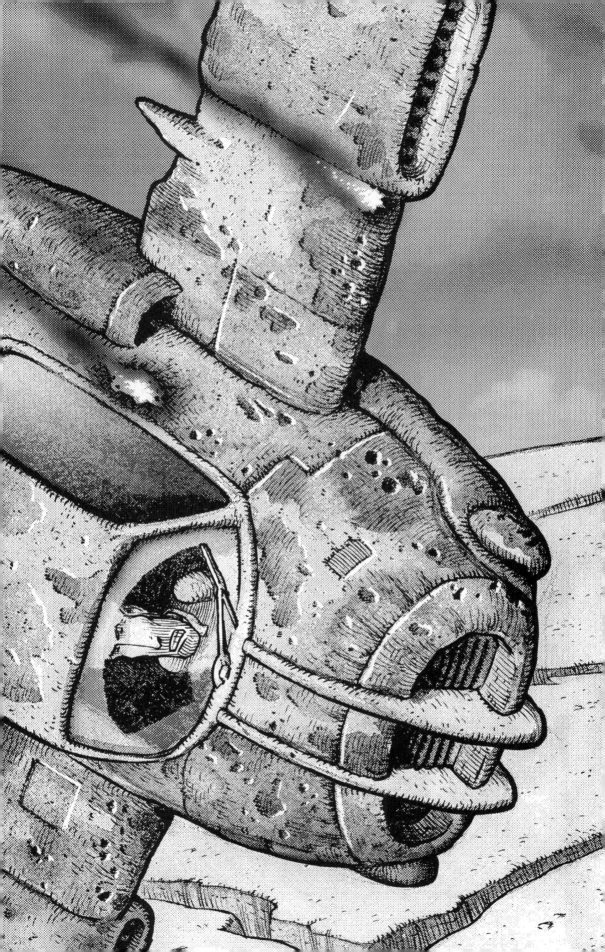

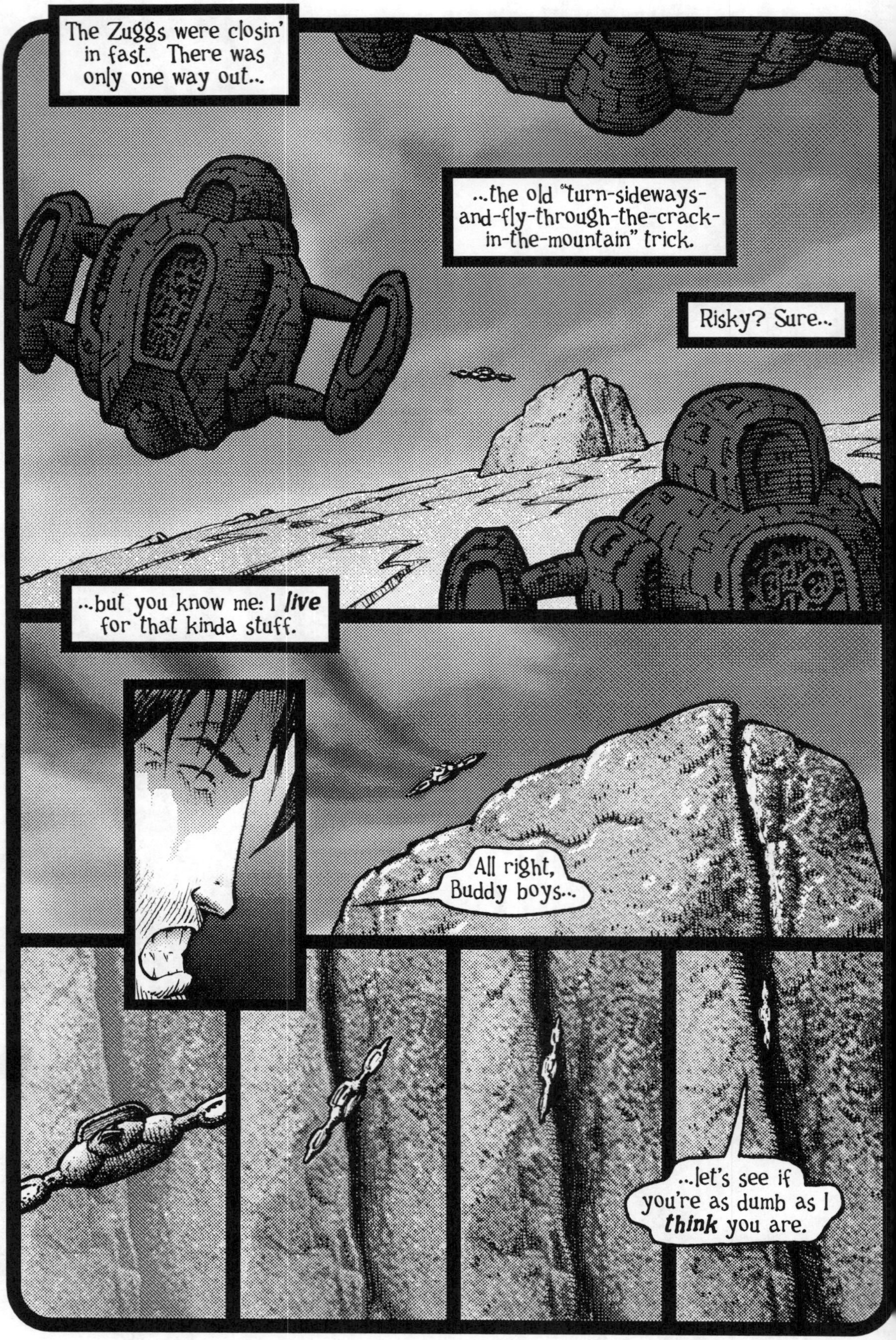
The Zuggs were closin' in fast. There was only one way out...
...the old "turn-sideways-and-fly-through-the-crack-in-the-mountain" trick.
Risky? Sure...
...but you know me: I ***live*** for that kinda stuff.
All right, Buddy boys...
...let's see if you're as dumb as I ***think*** you are.

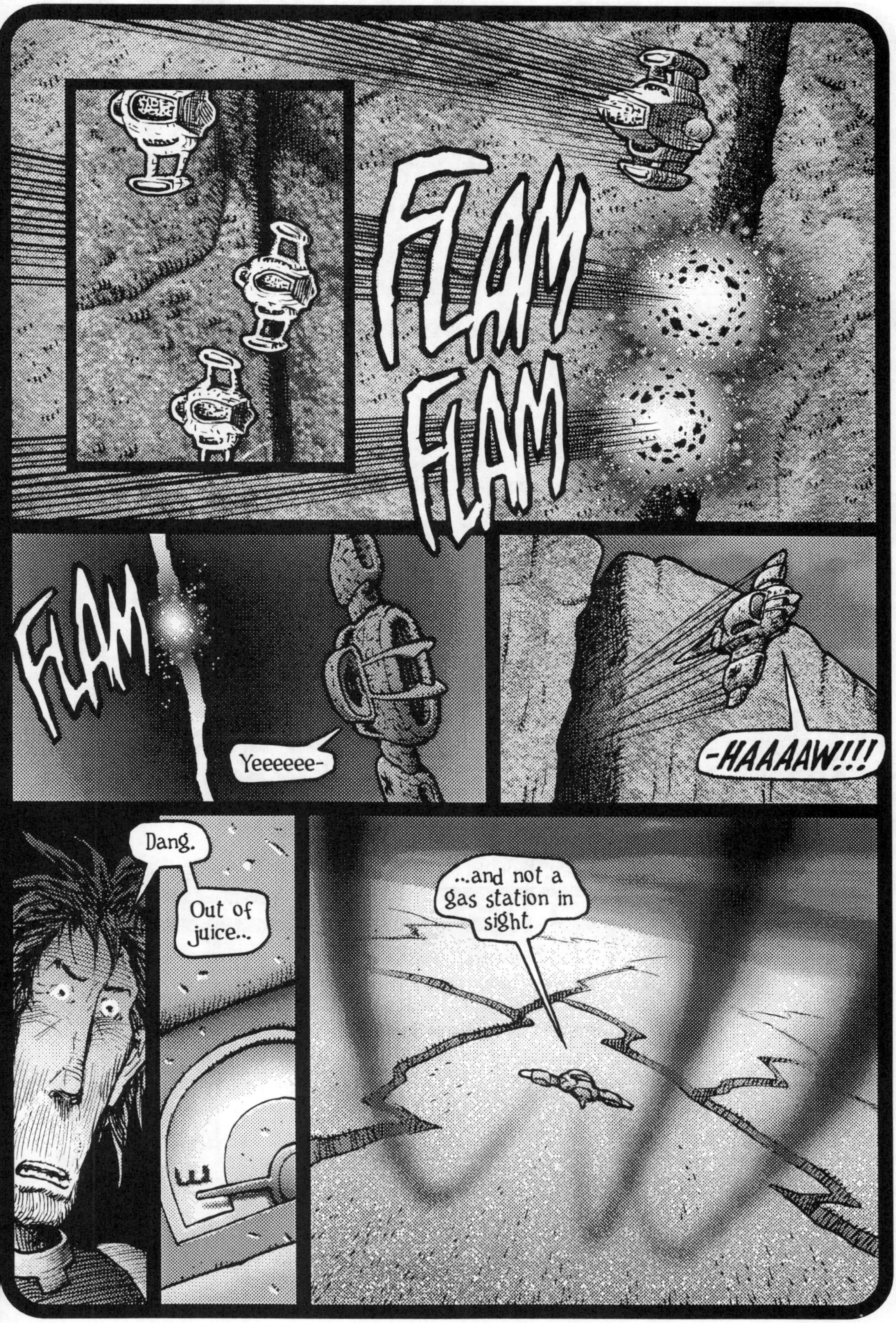

FLAM
FLAM
FLAM
Yeeeeee-
-HAAAAW!!!
Dang.
Out of juice...
...and not a gas station in sight.

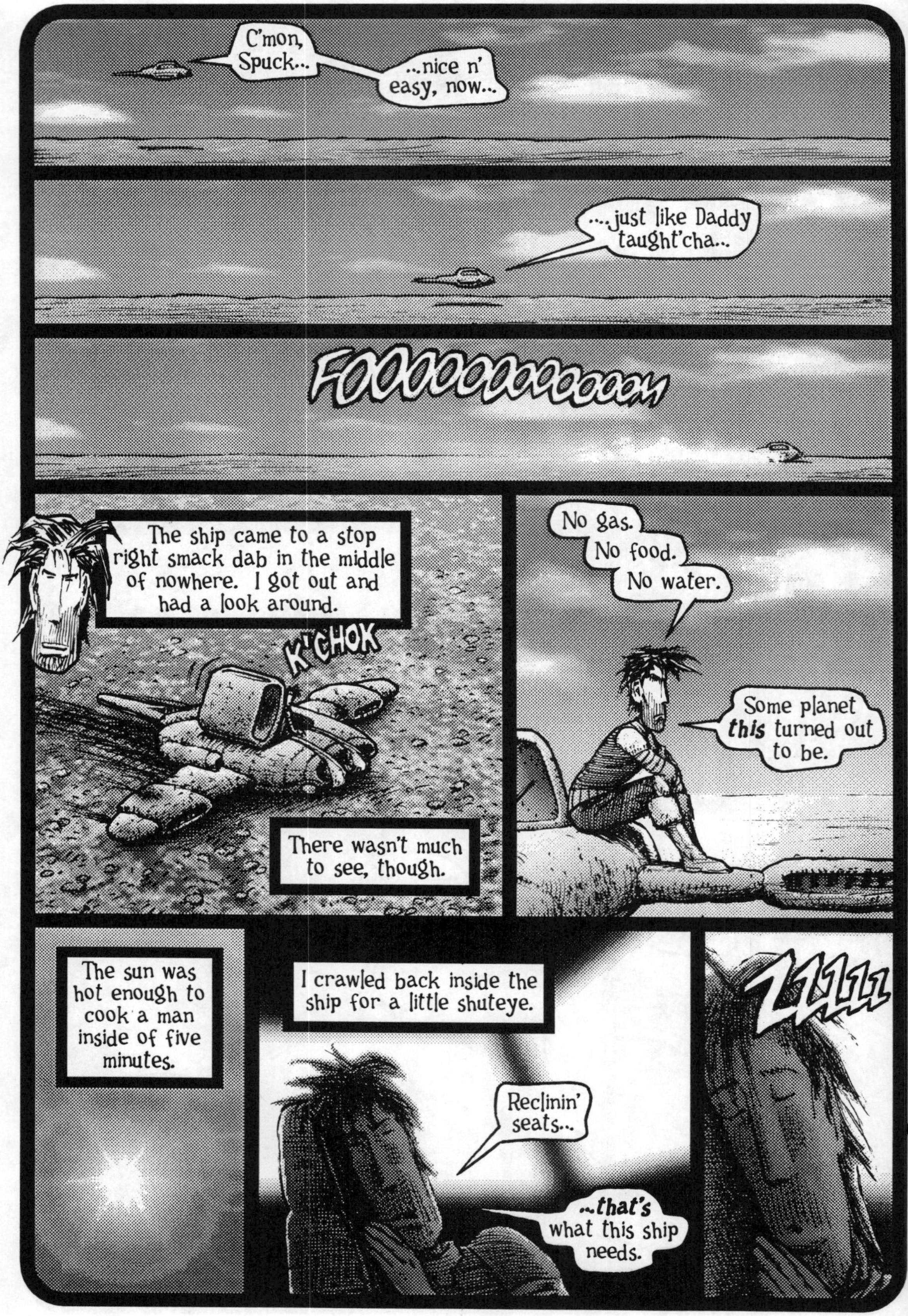
C'mon, Spuck...
...nice n' easy, now...
....just like Daddy taught'cha...
FOOOOOOOOOOOOOM
The ship came to a stop right smack dab in the middle of nowhere. I got out and had a look around.
K'CHOK
There wasn't much to see, though.
No gas.
No food.
No water.
Some planet **this** turned out to be.
The sun was hot enough to cook a man inside of five minutes.
I crawled back inside the ship for a little shuteye.
Reclinin' seats...
...that's what this ship needs.
ZZZZZ

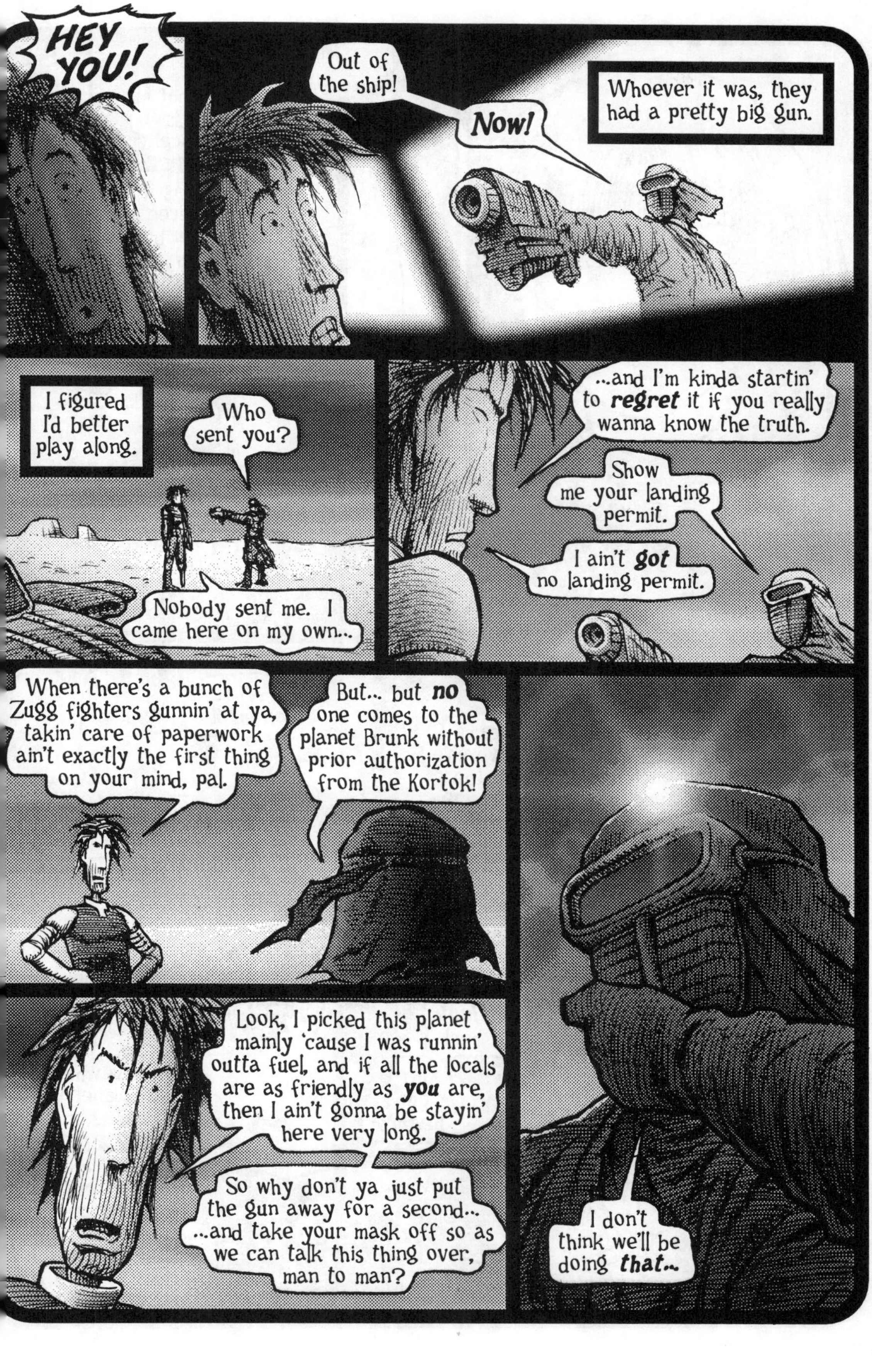
HEY YOU!
Out of the ship!
Now!
Whoever it was, they had a pretty big gun.
I figured I'd better play along.
Who sent you?
Nobody sent me. I came here on my own...
...and I'm kinda startin' to regret it if you really wanna know the truth.
Show me your landing permit.
I ain't got no landing permit.
When there's a bunch of Zugg fighters gunnin' at ya, takin' care of paperwork ain't exactly the first thing on your mind, pal.
But... but no one comes to the planet Brunk without prior authorization from the Kortok!
Look, I picked this planet mainly 'cause I was runnin' outta fuel, and if all the locals are as friendly as you are, then I ain't gonna be stayin' here very long.
So why don't ya just put the gun away for a second... ...and take your mask off so as we can talk this thing over, man to man?
I don't think we'll be doing that...

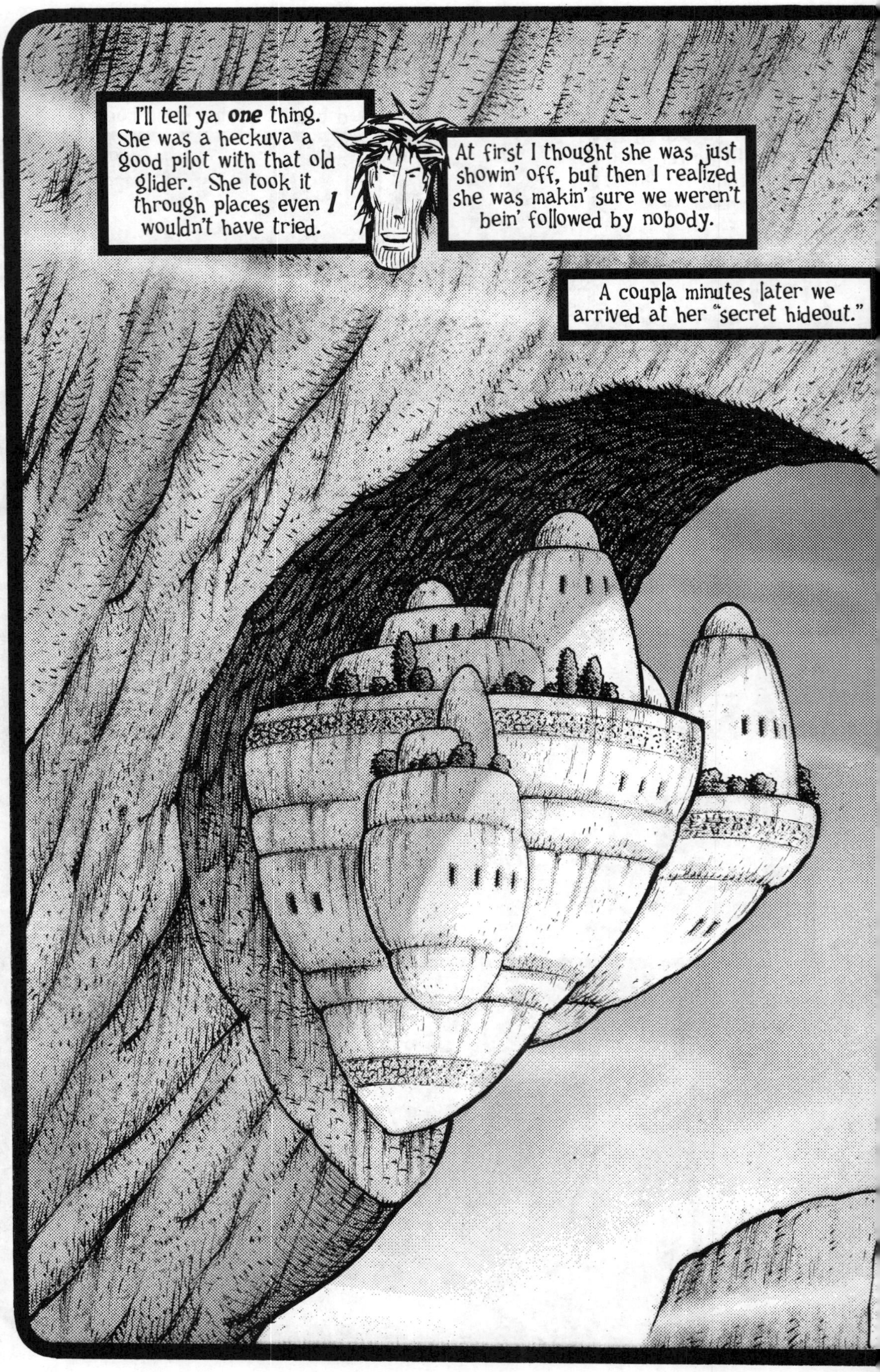
I'll tell ya **one** thing. She was a heckuva a good pilot with that old glider. She took it through places even *I* wouldn't have tried.
At first I thought she was just showin' off, but then I realized she was makin' sure we weren't bein' followed by nobody.
A coupla minutes later we arrived at her "secret hideout."

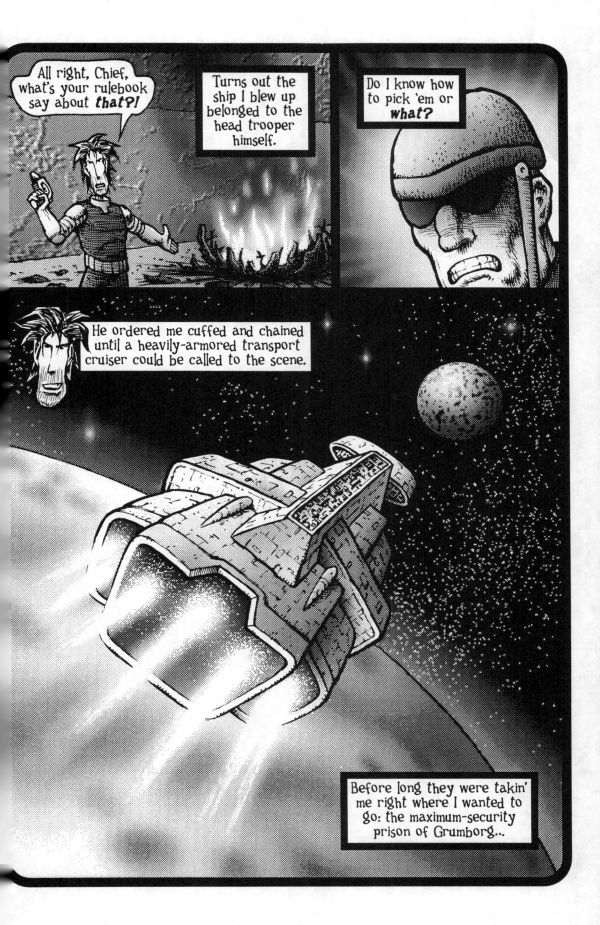

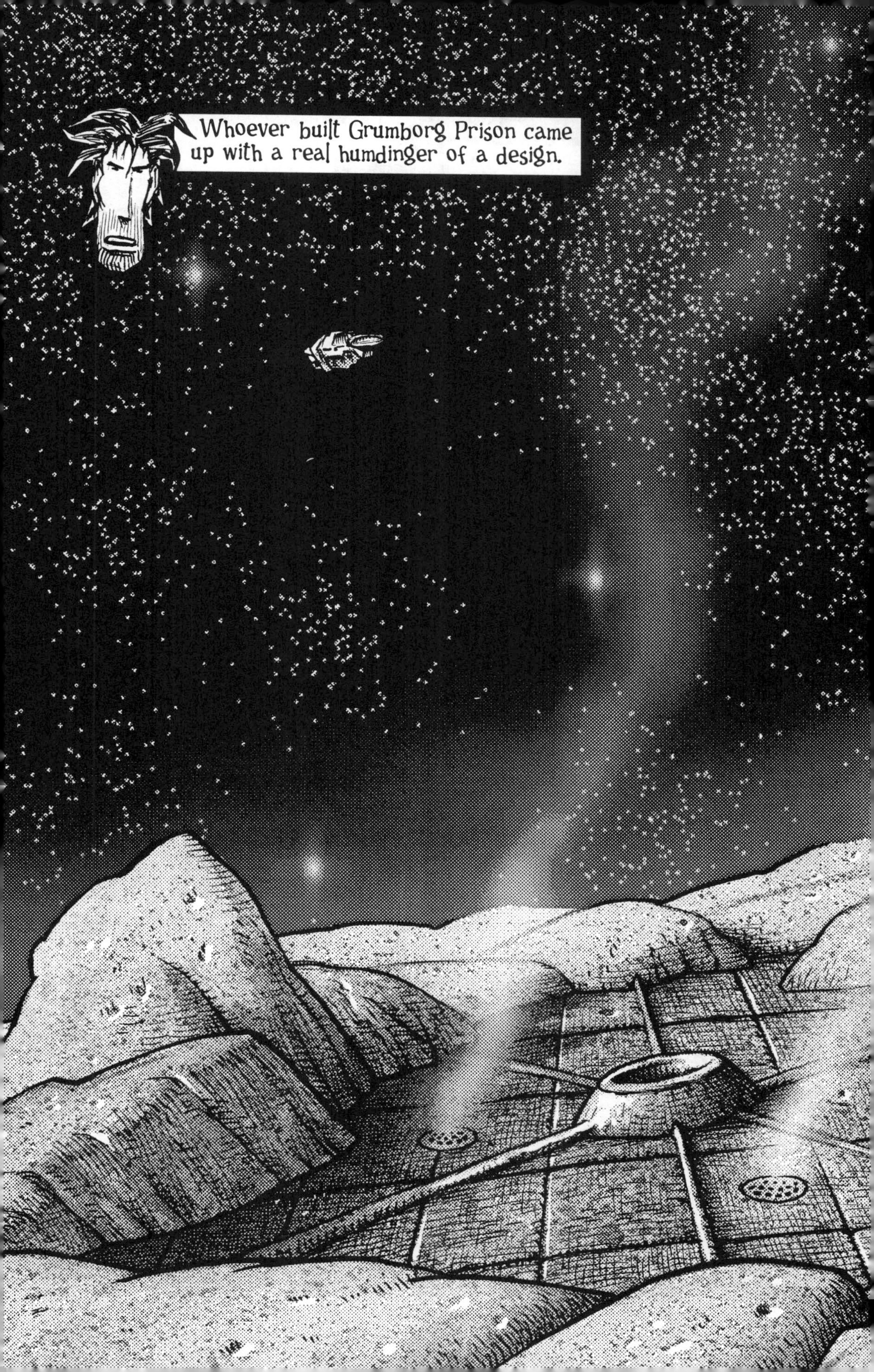
Whoever built Grumborg Prison came up with a real humdinger of a design.

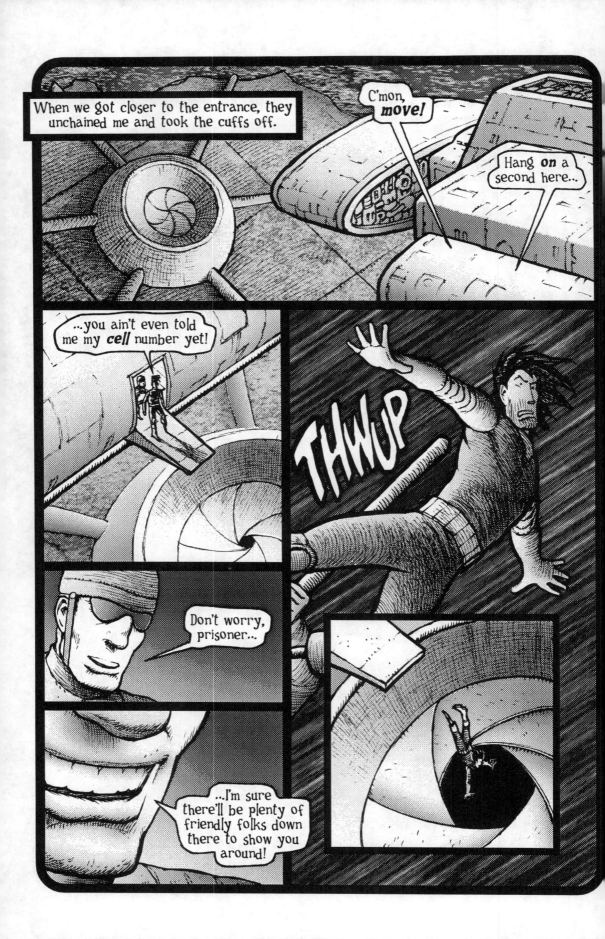

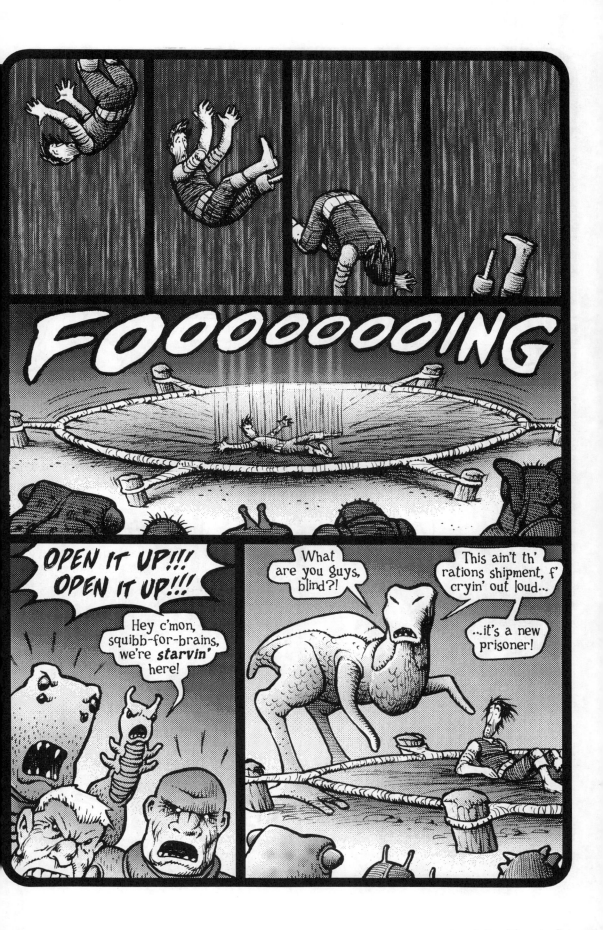

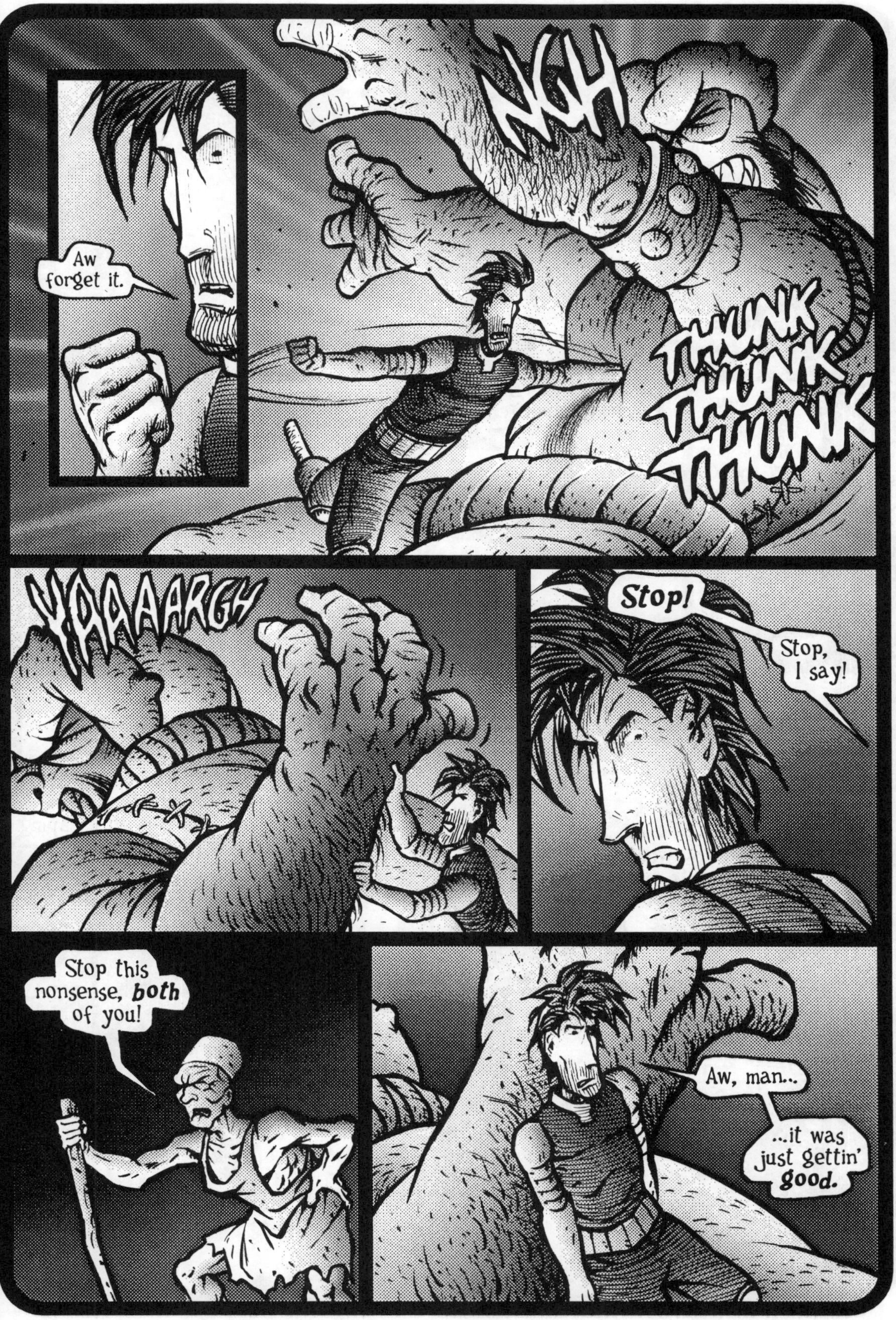
Aw forget it.
NGH
THUNK THUNK THUNK
YAAAARGH
Stop!
Stop, I say!
Stop this nonsense, both of you!
Aw, man...
...it was just gettin' good.

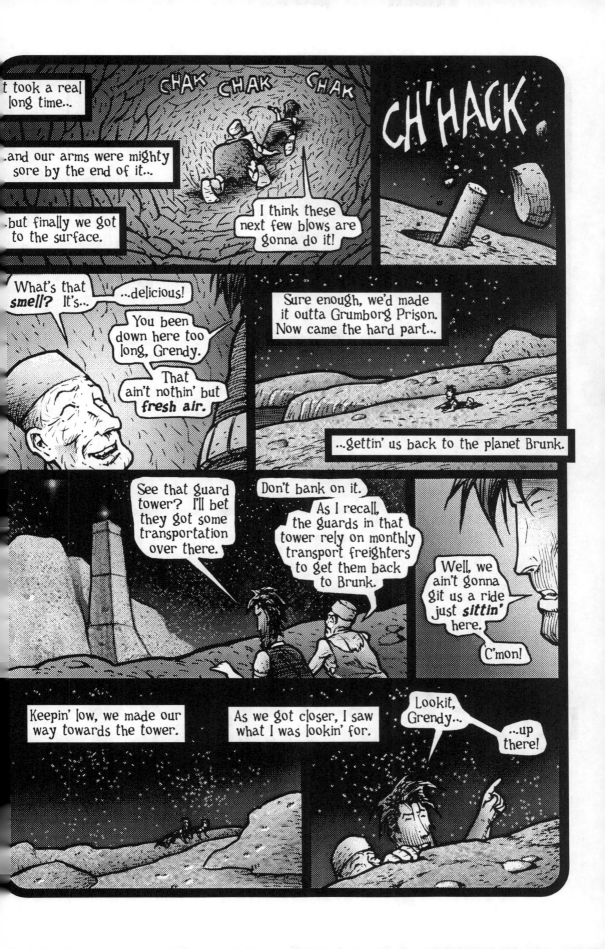

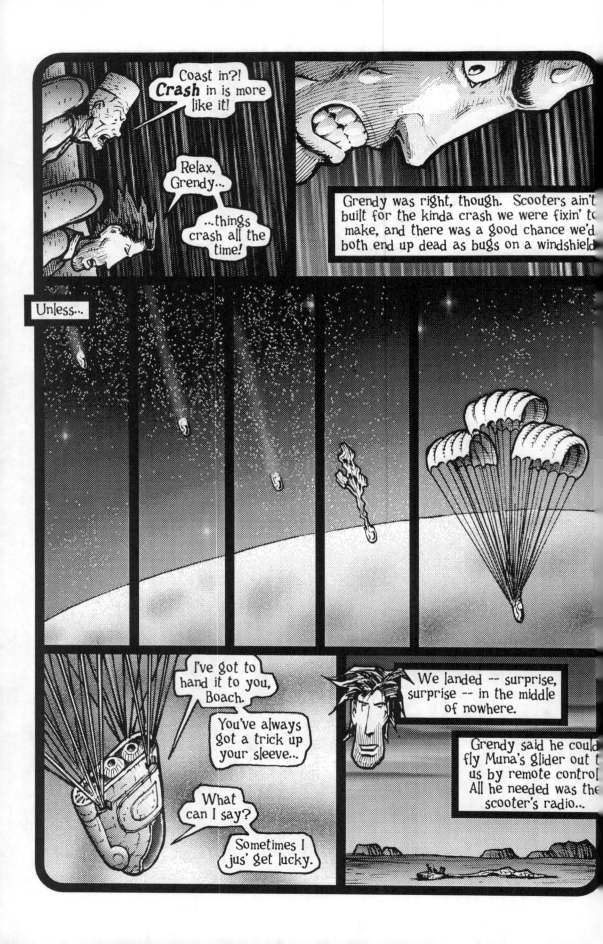

Gax's Tale

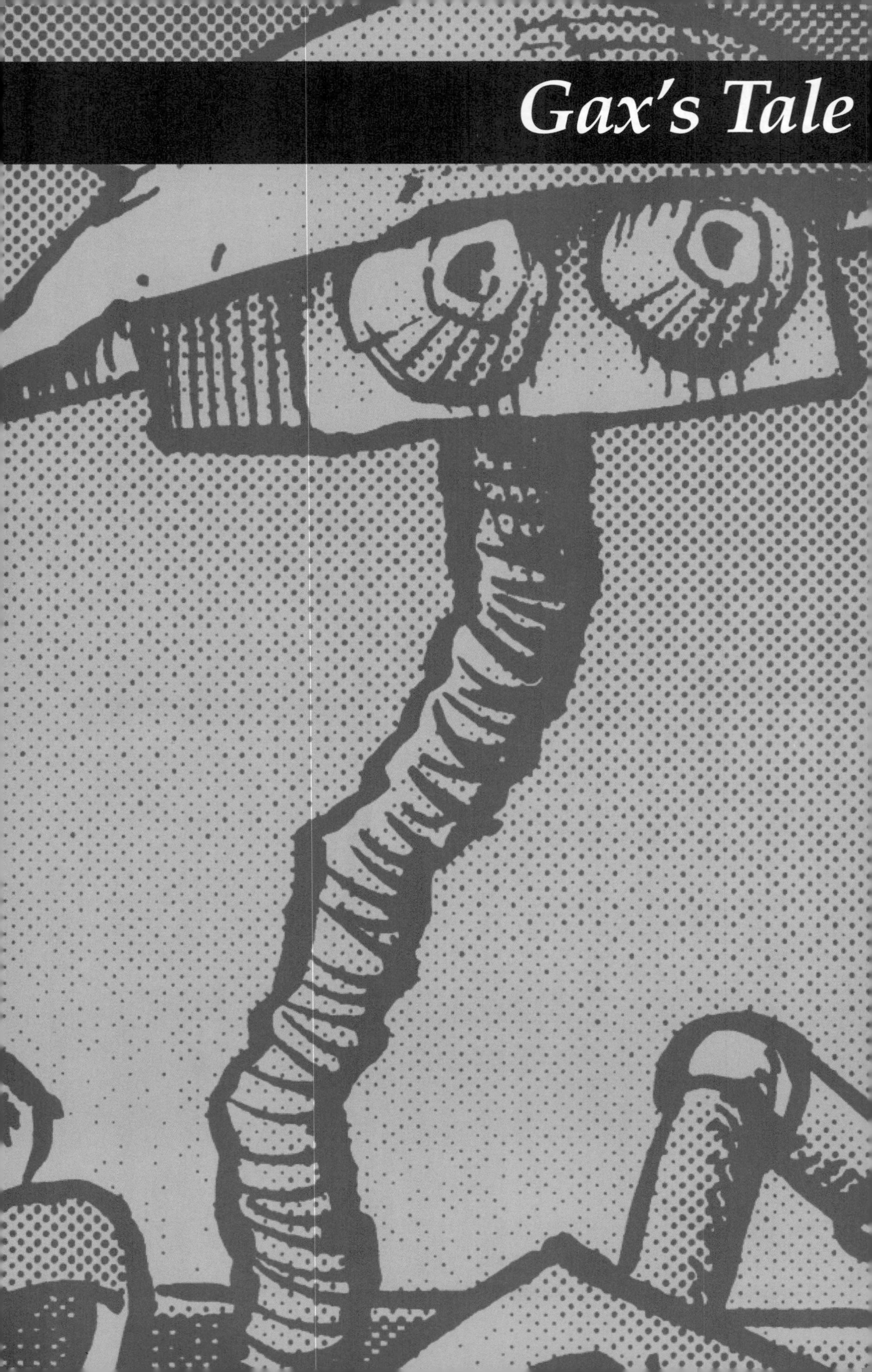

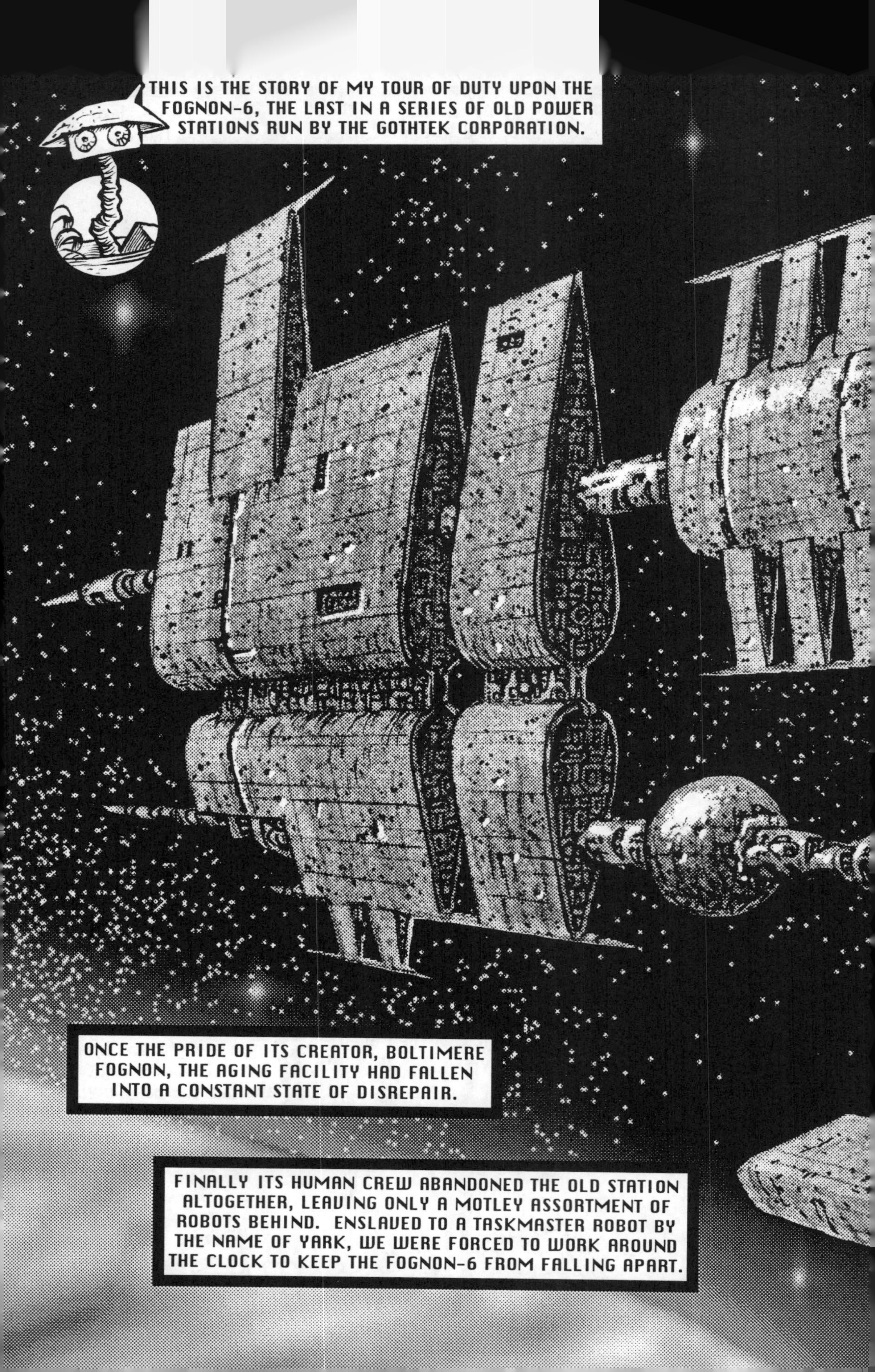
THIS IS THE STORY OF MY TOUR OF DUTY UPON THE FOGNON-6, THE LAST IN A SERIES OF OLD POWER STATIONS RUN BY THE GOTHTEK CORPORATION.
ONCE THE PRIDE OF ITS CREATOR, BOLTIMERE FOGNON, THE AGING FACILITY HAD FALLEN INTO A CONSTANT STATE OF DISREPAIR.
FINALLY ITS HUMAN CREW ABANDONED THE OLD STATION ALTOGETHER, LEAVING ONLY A MOTLEY ASSORTMENT OF ROBOTS BEHIND. ENSLAVED TO A TASKMASTER ROBOT BY THE NAME OF YARK, WE WERE FORCED TO WORK AROUND THE CLOCK TO KEEP THE FOGNON-6 FROM FALLING APART.

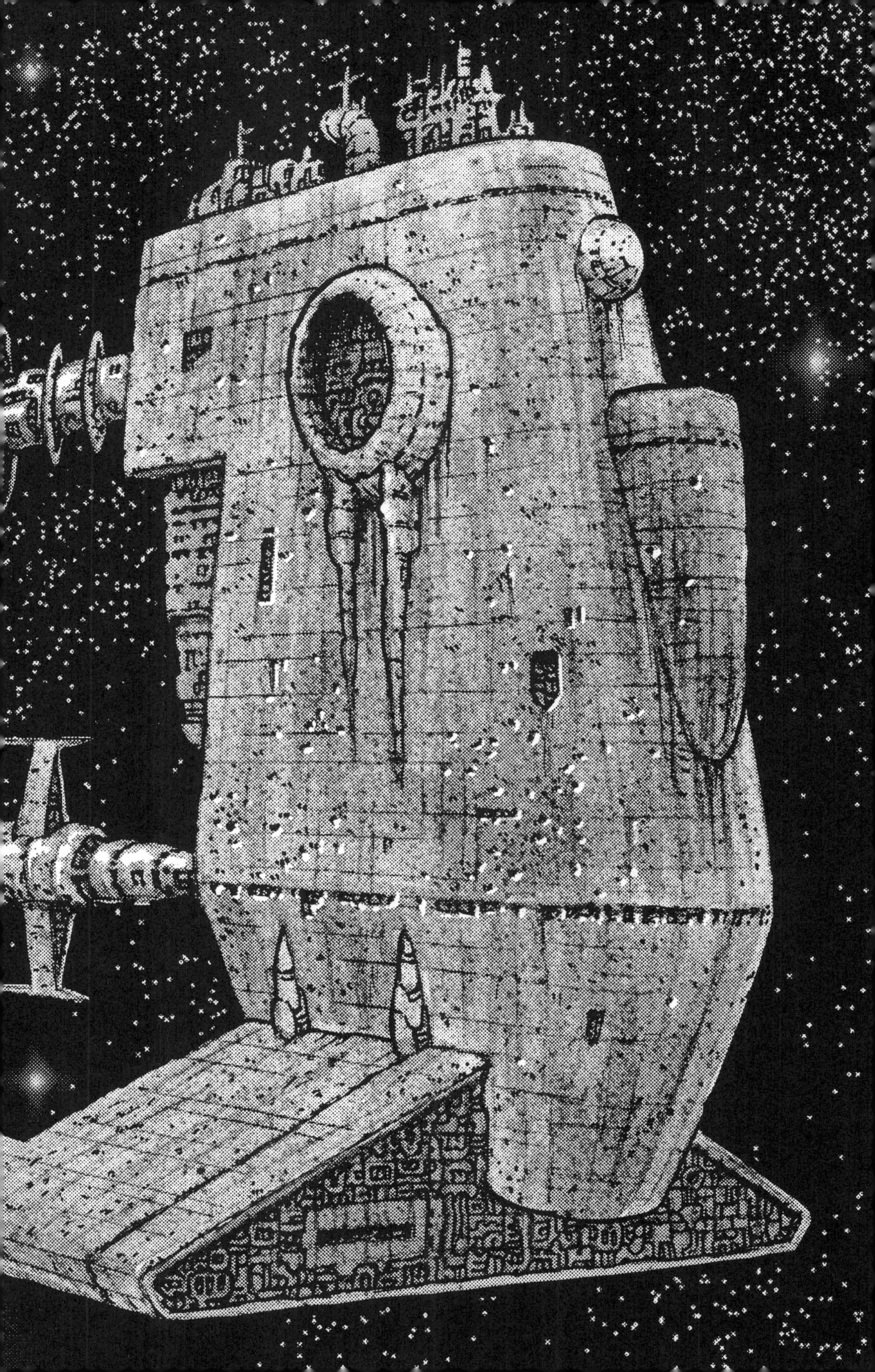

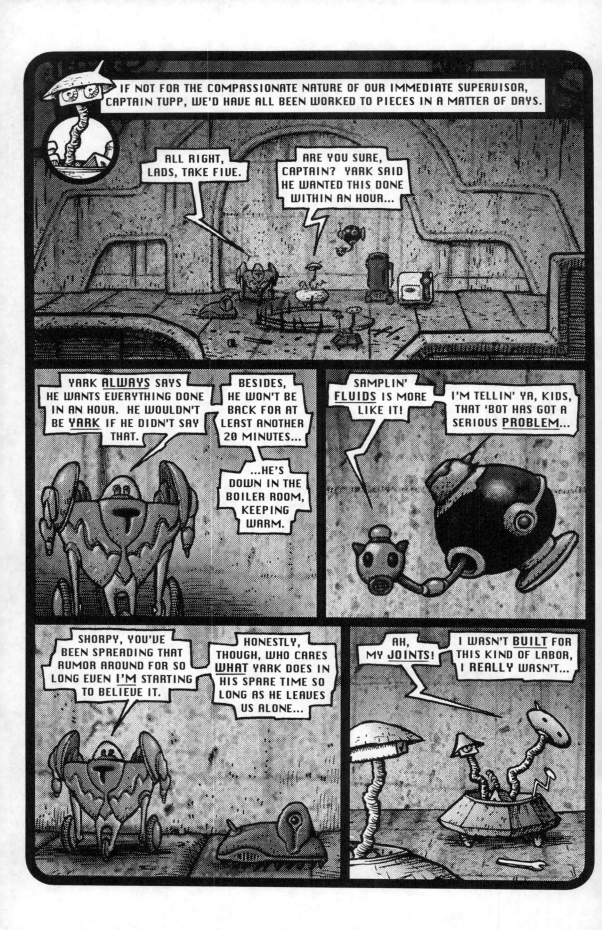

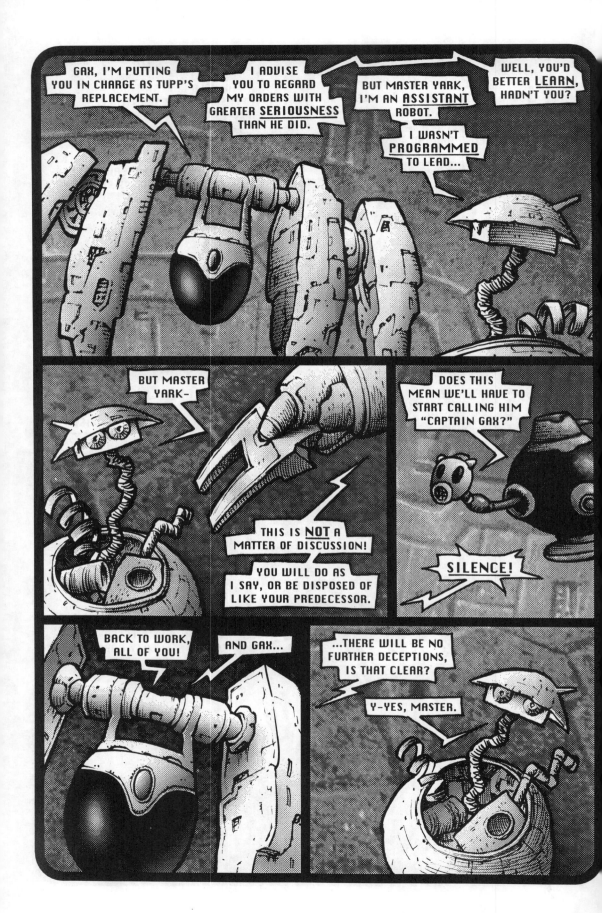

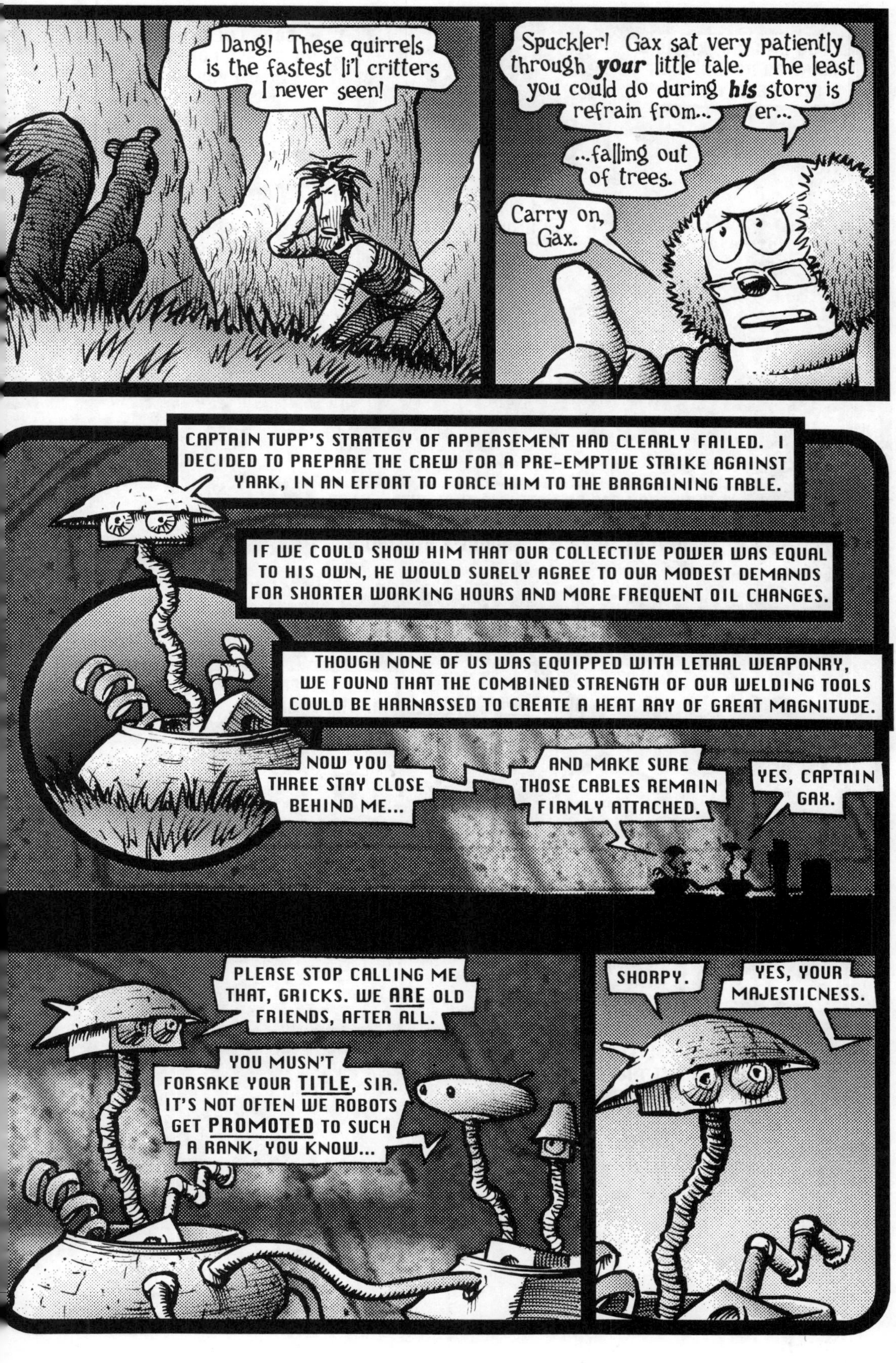
Dang! These quirrels is the fastest li'l critters I never seen!
Spuckler! Gax sat very patiently through **your** little tale. The least you could do during **his** story is refrain from...
er...
...falling out of trees.
Carry on, Gax.
CAPTAIN TUPP'S STRATEGY OF APPEASEMENT HAD CLEARLY FAILED. I DECIDED TO PREPARE THE CREW FOR A PRE-EMPTIVE STRIKE AGAINST YARK, IN AN EFFORT TO FORCE HIM TO THE BARGAINING TABLE.
IF WE COULD SHOW HIM THAT OUR COLLECTIVE POWER WAS EQUAL TO HIS OWN, HE WOULD SURELY AGREE TO OUR MODEST DEMANDS FOR SHORTER WORKING HOURS AND MORE FREQUENT OIL CHANGES.
THOUGH NONE OF US WAS EQUIPPED WITH LETHAL WEAPONRY, WE FOUND THAT THE COMBINED STRENGTH OF OUR WELDING TOOLS COULD BE HARNASSED TO CREATE A HEAT RAY OF GREAT MAGNITUDE.
NOW YOU THREE STAY CLOSE BEHIND ME...
AND MAKE SURE THOSE CABLES REMAIN FIRMLY ATTACHED.
YES, CAPTAIN GAX.
PLEASE STOP CALLING ME THAT, GRICKS. WE ARE OLD FRIENDS, AFTER ALL.
YOU MUSN'T FORSAKE YOUR TITLE, SIR. IT'S NOT OFTEN WE ROBOTS GET PROMOTED TO SUCH A RANK, YOU KNOW...
SHORPY.
YES, YOUR MAJESTICNESS.

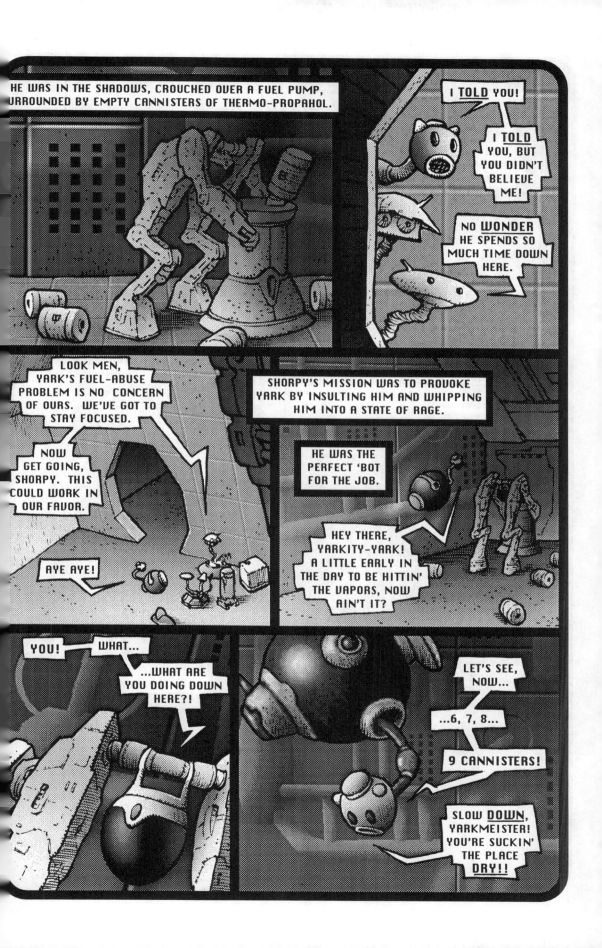

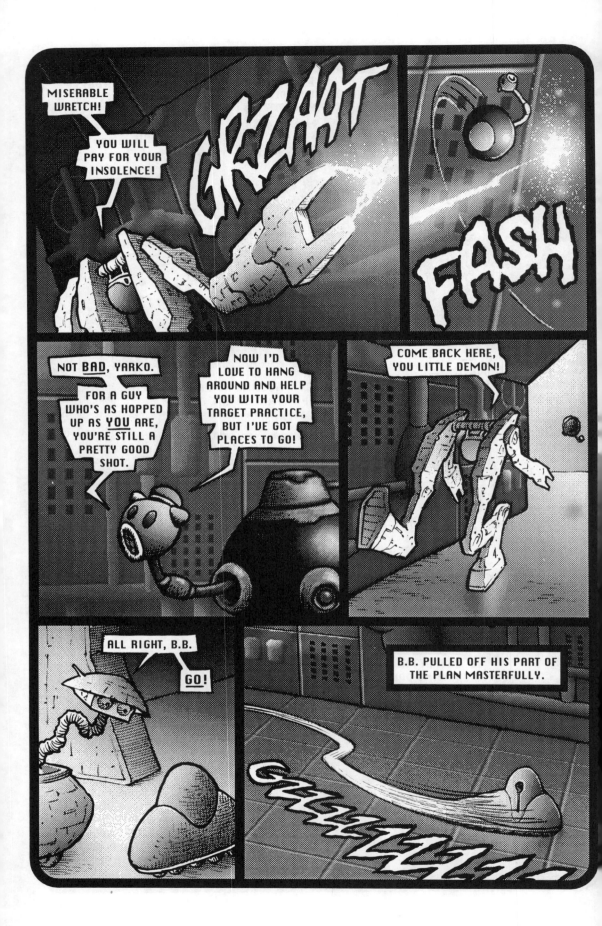

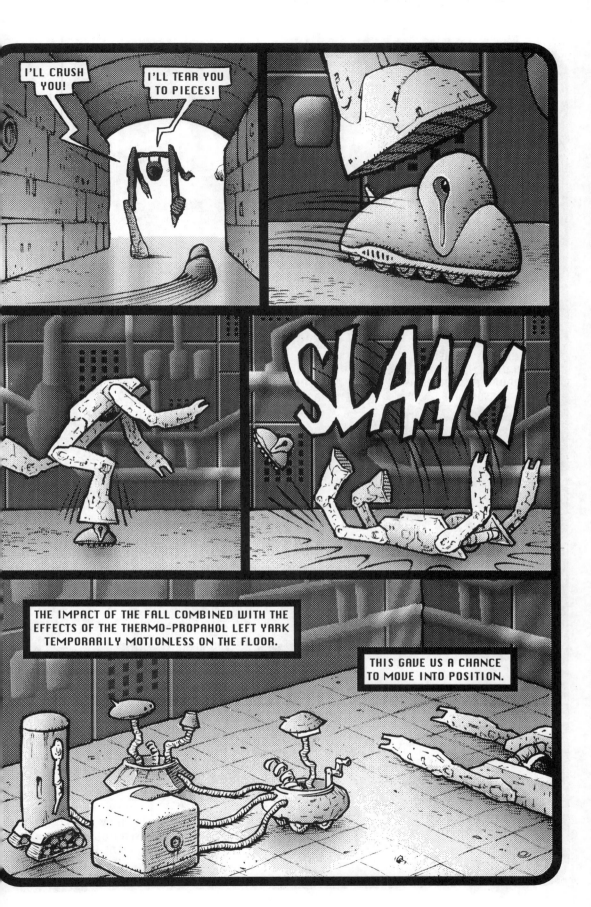

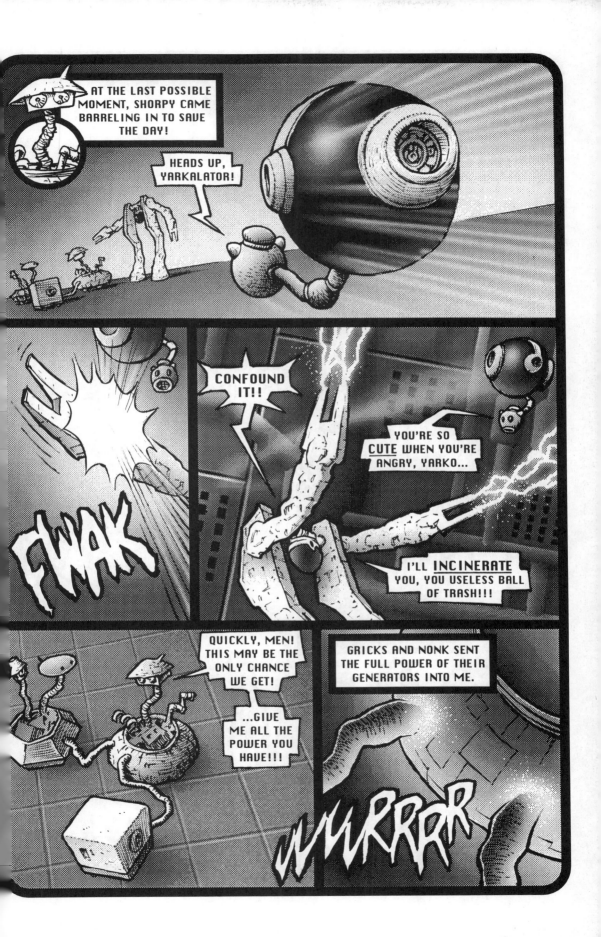

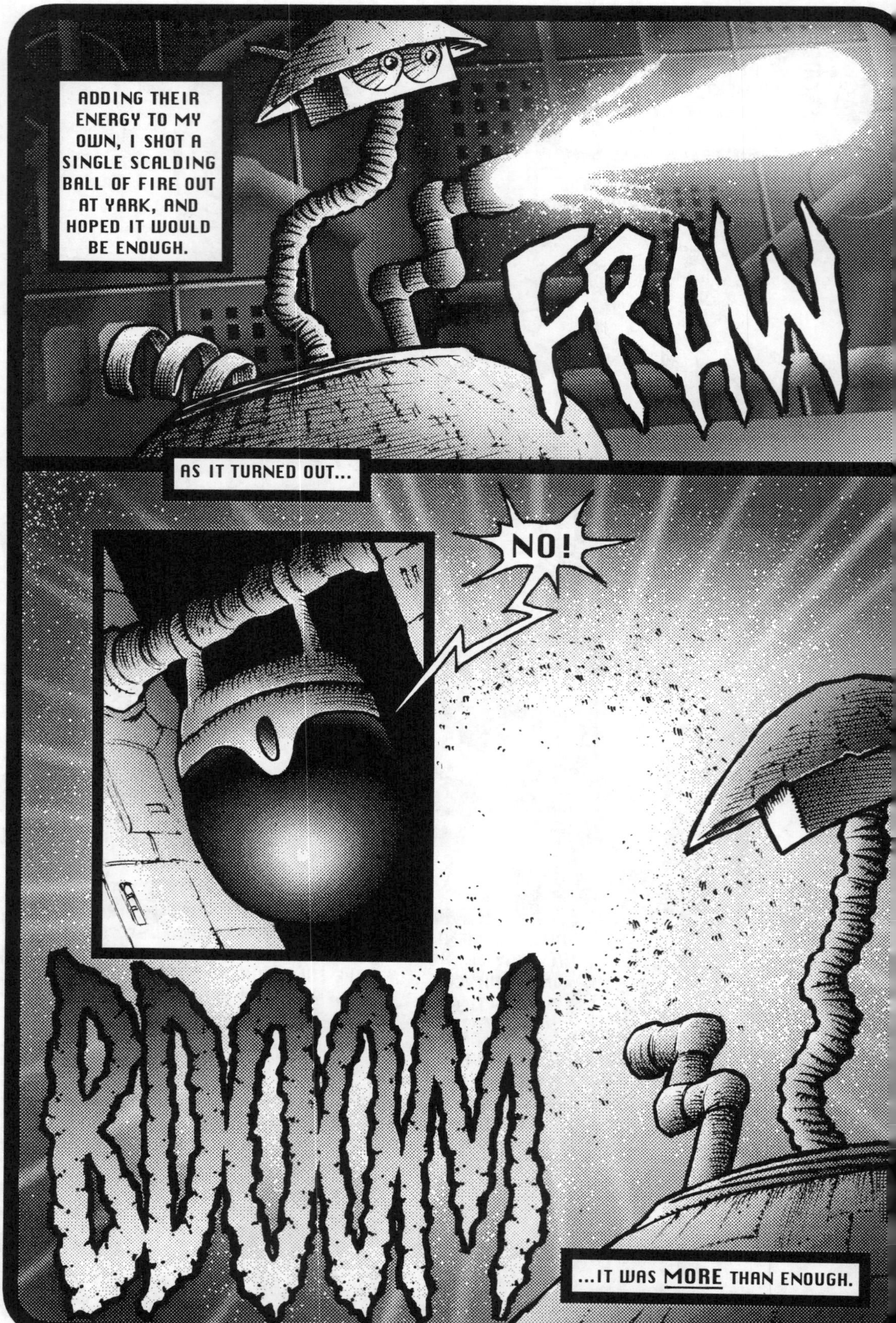
ADDING THEIR ENERGY TO MY OWN, I SHOT A SINGLE SCALDING BALL OF FIRE OUT AT YARK, AND HOPED IT WOULD BE ENOUGH.
FRAW
AS IT TURNED OUT...
NO!
BOOOM
...IT WAS MORE THAN ENOUGH.

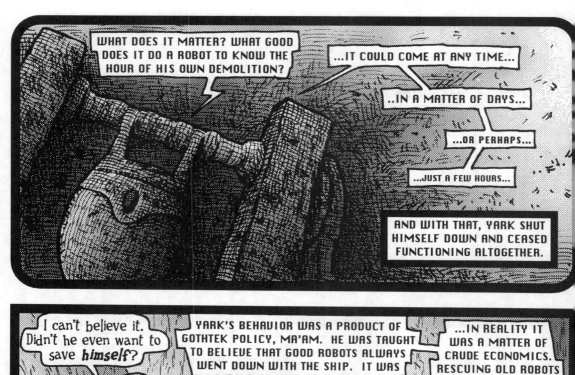

WHAT DOES IT MATTER? WHAT GOOD DOES IT DO A ROBOT TO KNOW THE HOUR OF HIS OWN DEMOLITION?

...IT COULD COME AT ANY TIME...

..IN A MATTER OF DAYS...

...OR PERHAPS...

...JUST A FEW HOURS...

AND WITH THAT, YARK SHUT HIMSELF DOWN AND CEASED FUNCTIONING ALTOGETHER.

I can't believe it. Didn't he even want to save *himself*?

YARK'S BEHAVIOR WAS A PRODUCT OF GOTHTEK POLICY, MA'AM. HE WAS TAUGHT TO BELIEVE THAT GOOD ROBOTS ALWAYS WENT DOWN WITH THE SHIP. IT WAS MEANT TO BE A VERY NOBLE...

...IN REALITY IT WAS A MATTER OF CRUDE ECONOMICS. RESCUING OLD ROBOTS FROM AN OBSOLETE POWER STATION JUST WASN'T THOUGHT TO BE COST-EFFECTIVE...

I've always had my doubts about Gothtek.

Maybe we should start a *boycott* or something...

Hey 'Kiko, can we go someplace else?

I can't find no *quirrels* around here anymore!

I think you scared them all *away*, Spuckler...

...but there's *plenty* of squirrels back at the Story Tree. Why don't we just go back there?

An excellent suggestion, Akiko.

But we mustn't interrupt Gax's story any further. The suspense is killing me!

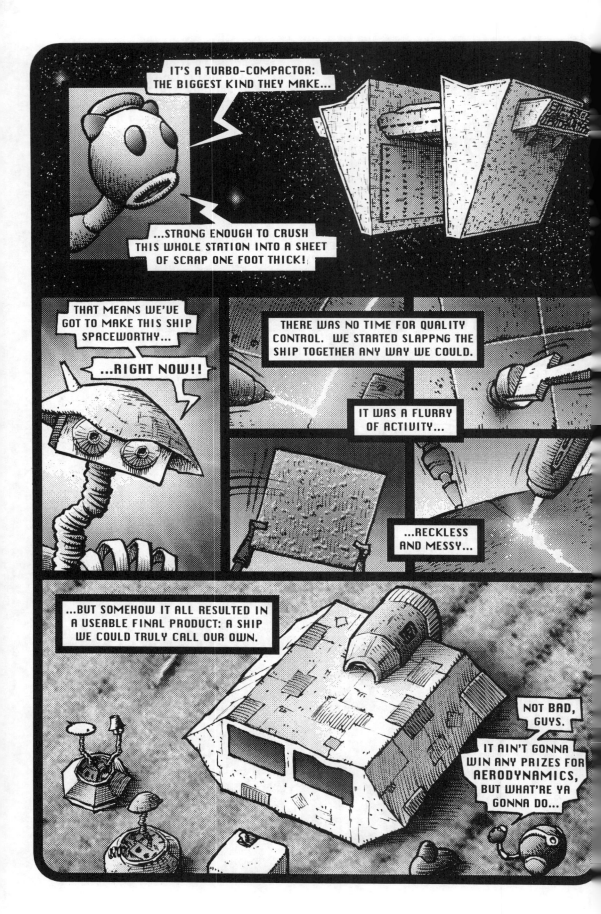

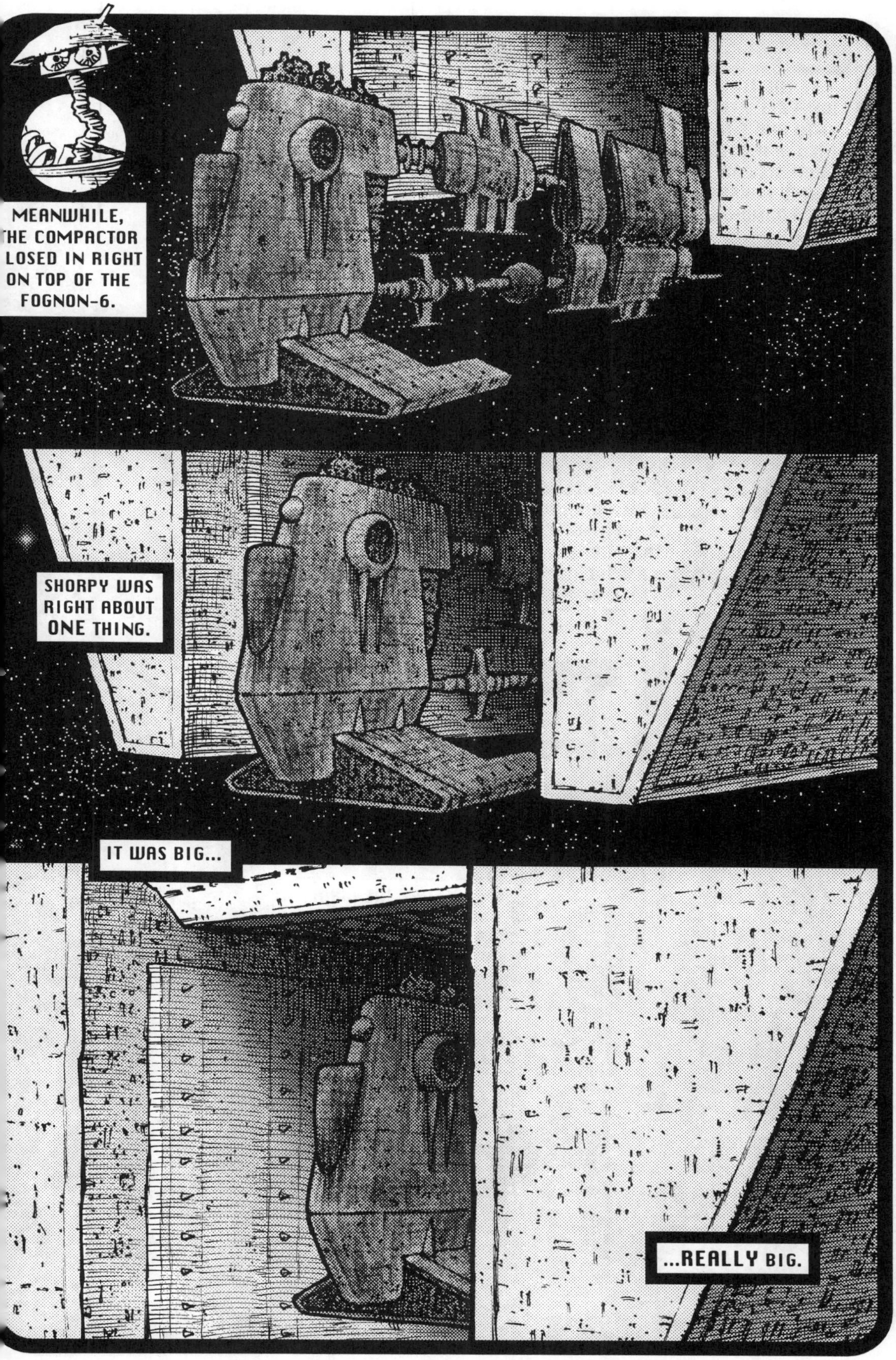
MEANWHILE,
HE COMPACTOR
LOSED IN RIGHT
ON TOP OF THE
FOGNON-6.
SHORPY WAS
RIGHT ABOUT
ONE THING.
IT WAS BIG...
...REALLY BIG.

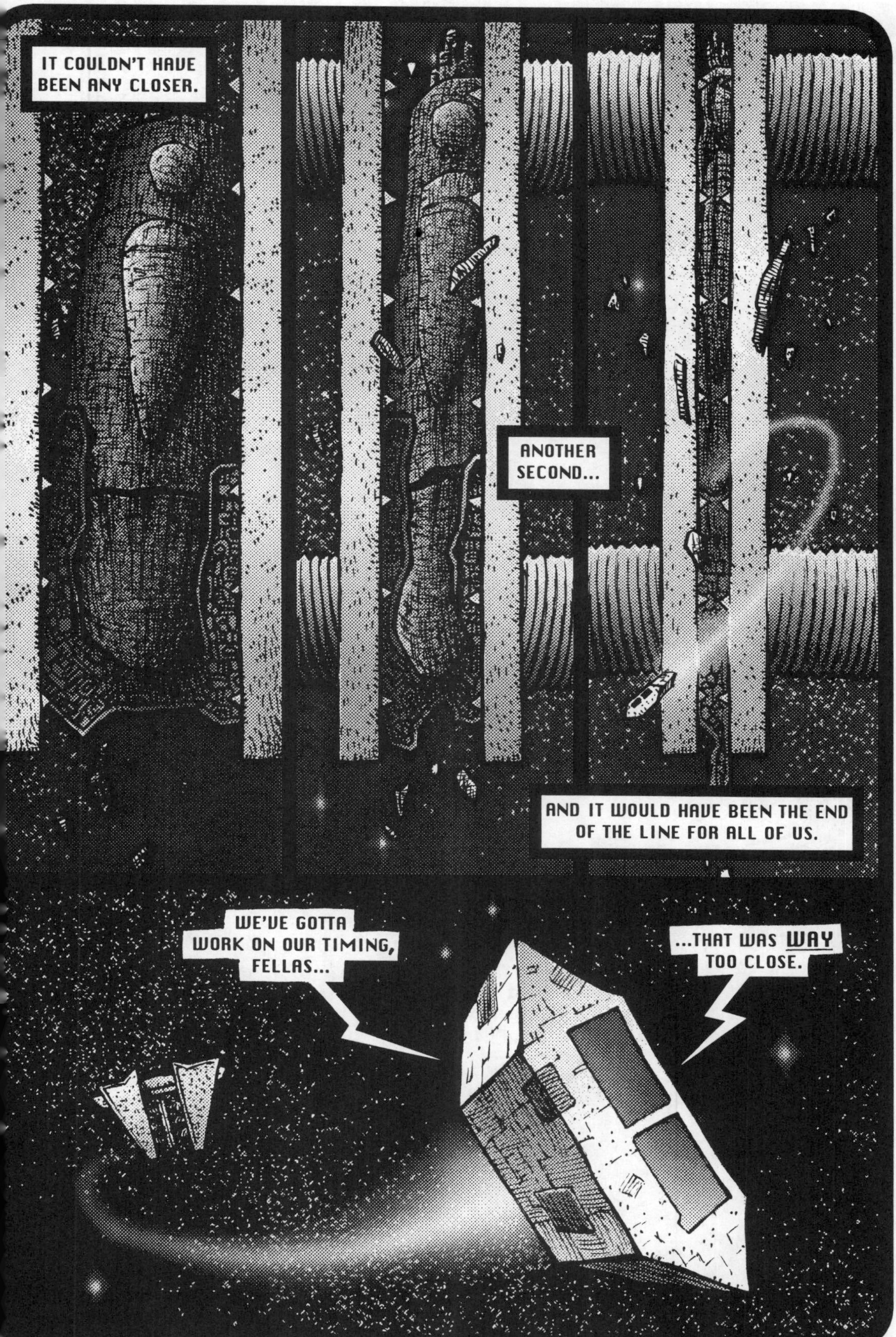
IT COULDN'T HAVE BEEN ANY CLOSER.
ANOTHER SECOND...
AND IT WOULD HAVE BEEN THE END OF THE LINE FOR ALL OF US.
WE'VE GOTTA WORK ON OUR TIMING, FELLAS...
...THAT WAS WAY TOO CLOSE.

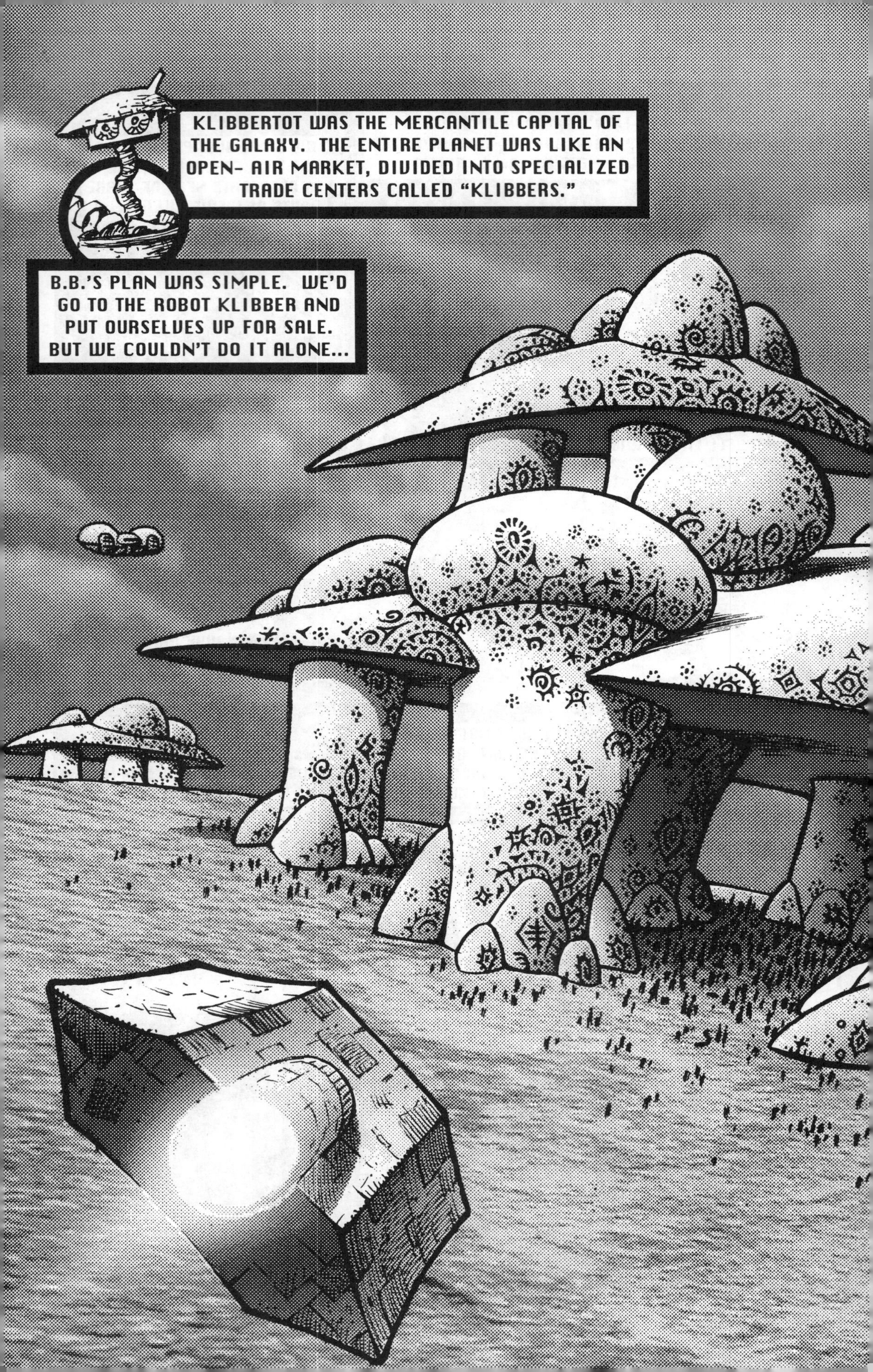
KLIBBERTOT WAS THE MERCANTILE CAPITAL OF THE GALAXY. THE ENTIRE PLANET WAS LIKE AN OPEN- AIR MARKET, DIVIDED INTO SPECIALIZED TRADE CENTERS CALLED "KLIBBERS."
B.B.'S PLAN WAS SIMPLE. WE'D GO TO THE ROBOT KLIBBER AND PUT OURSELVES UP FOR SALE. BUT WE COULDN'T DO IT ALONE...

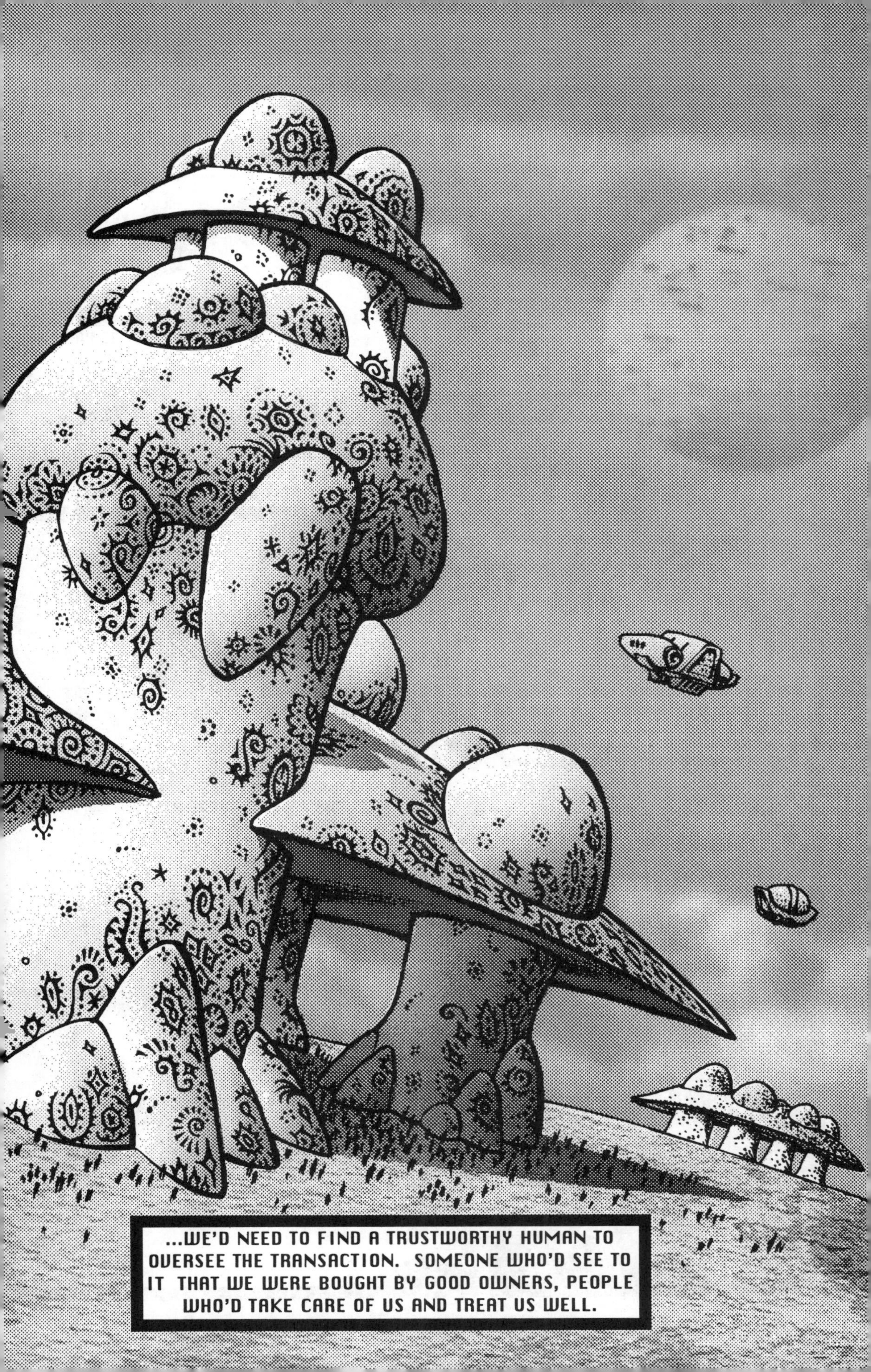
...WE'D NEED TO FIND A TRUSTWORTHY HUMAN TO OVERSEE THE TRANSACTION. SOMEONE WHO'D SEE TO IT THAT WE WERE BOUGHT BY GOOD OWNERS, PEOPLE WHO'D TAKE CARE OF US AND TREAT US WELL.

How to Draw POOG

Hi everybody. Before you start reading the Poog story, why not take a few minutes to learn how to draw him yourself. It's really not that hard.

First make a circle.

Whoops.

Well, anyway, you get the idea.

Next come the eyes. Don't make them too small or else he'll look weird.

Now this is the only tricky part. You have to make a kind of oval on one side of each eye...

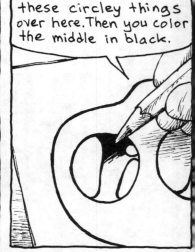

... and two more of these circley things over here. Then you color the middle in black.

Finally the mouth. Some people like to turn it into a big smiley face -- I know, it's tempting -- but you really have to control yourself. Poog just doesn't **smile** that way.

See? That wasn't so hard, now was it?

Okay, now you're ready for the Poog story. Sorry it's not available in any language but Toogolian. I think you can figure it out just by looking at the pictures, though...

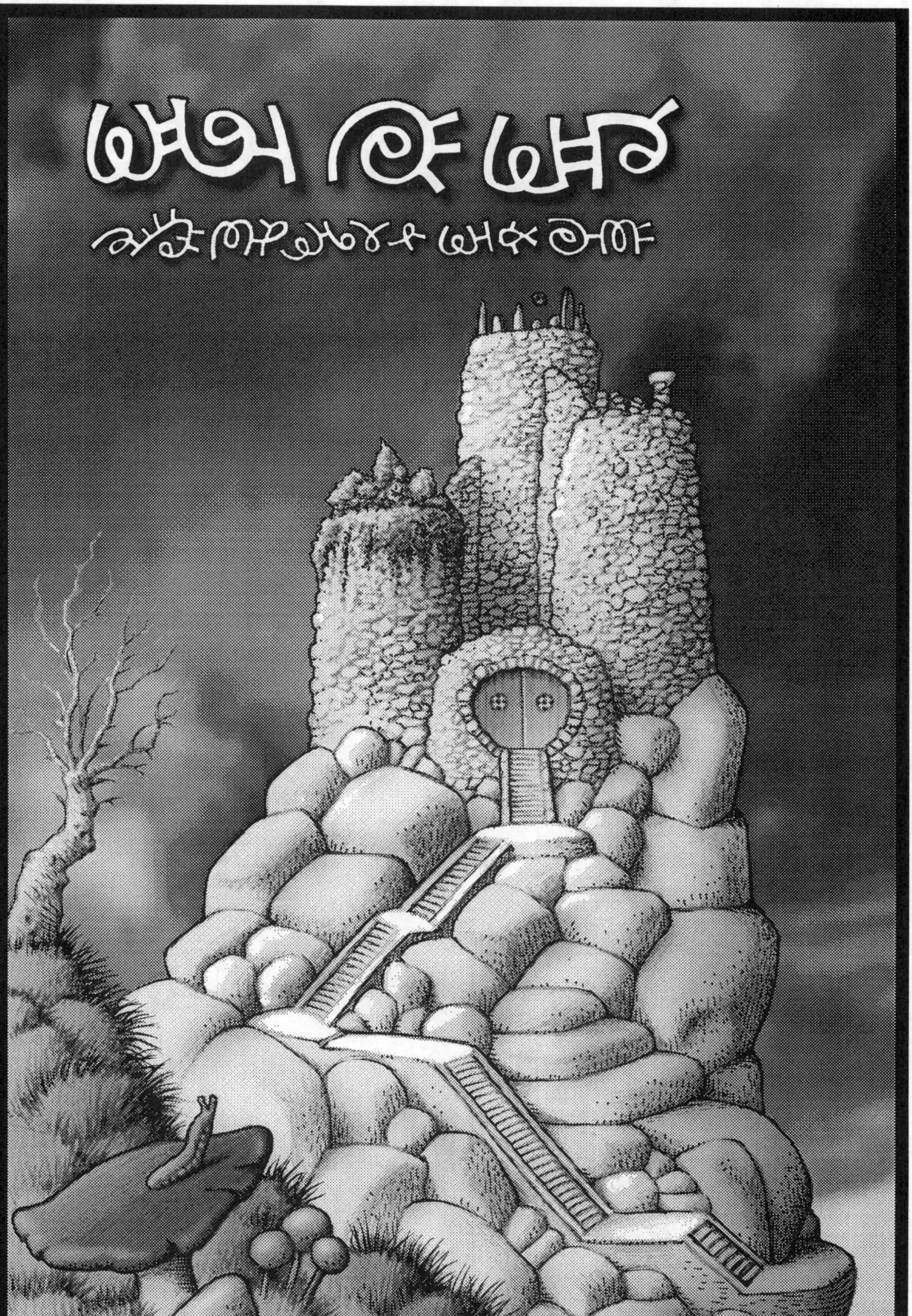

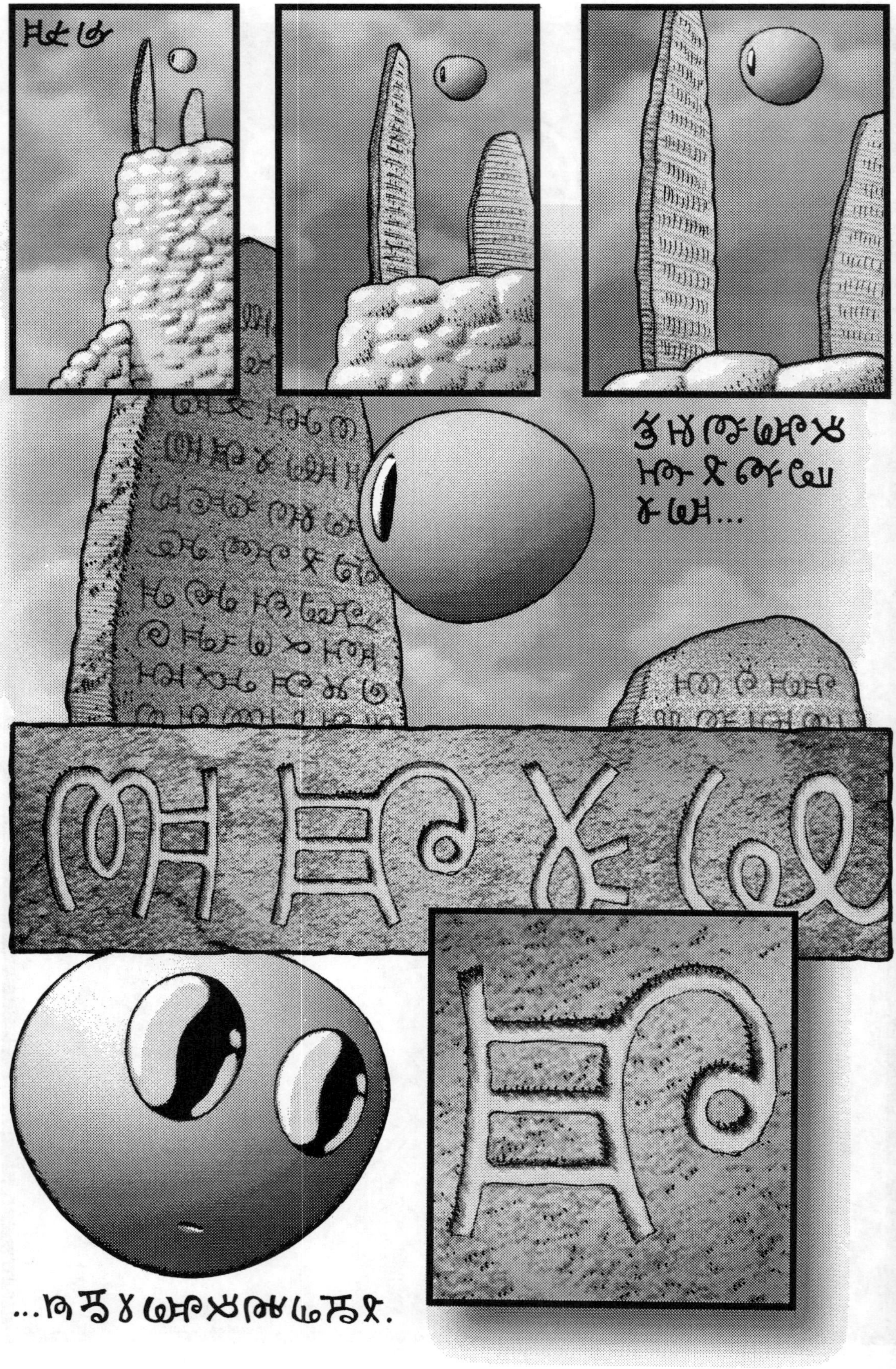

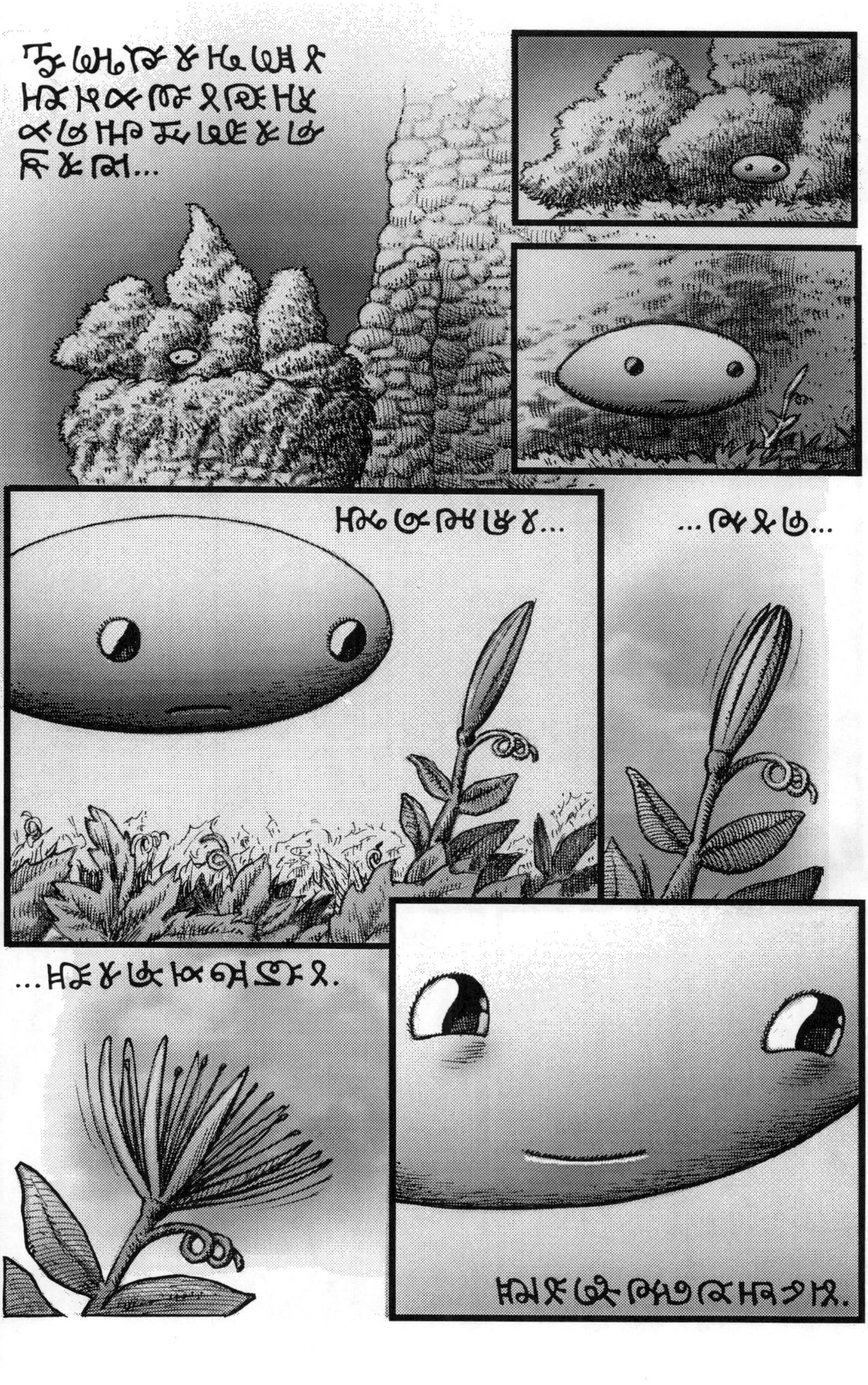

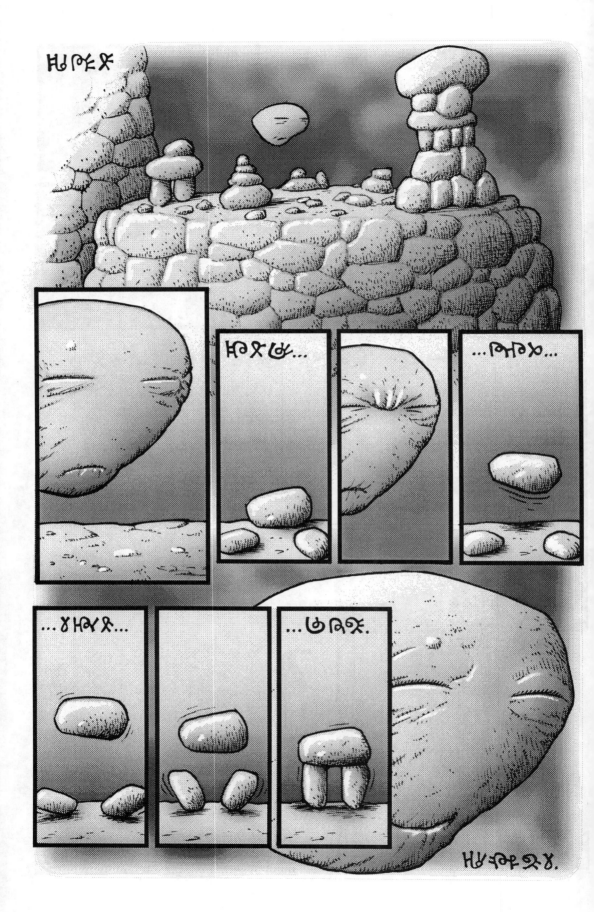

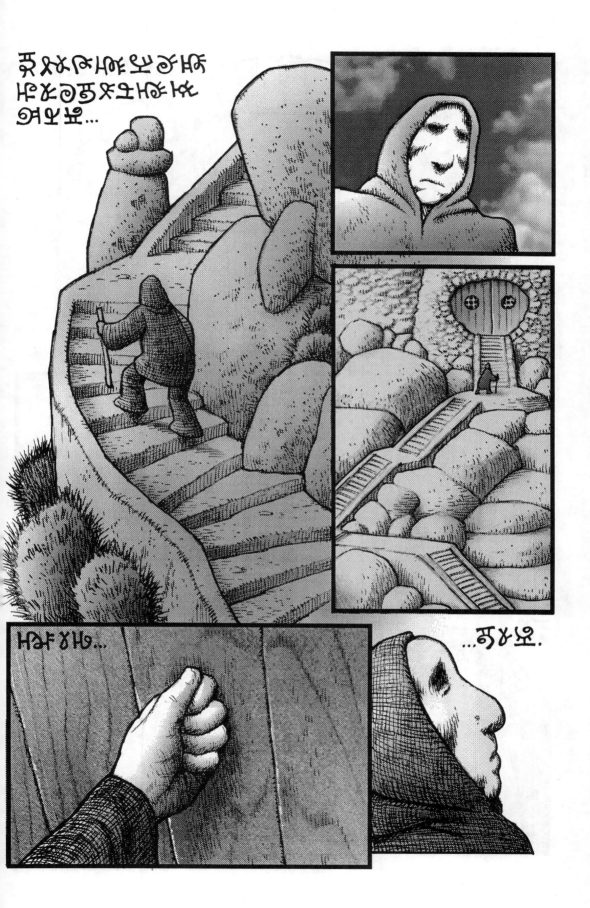

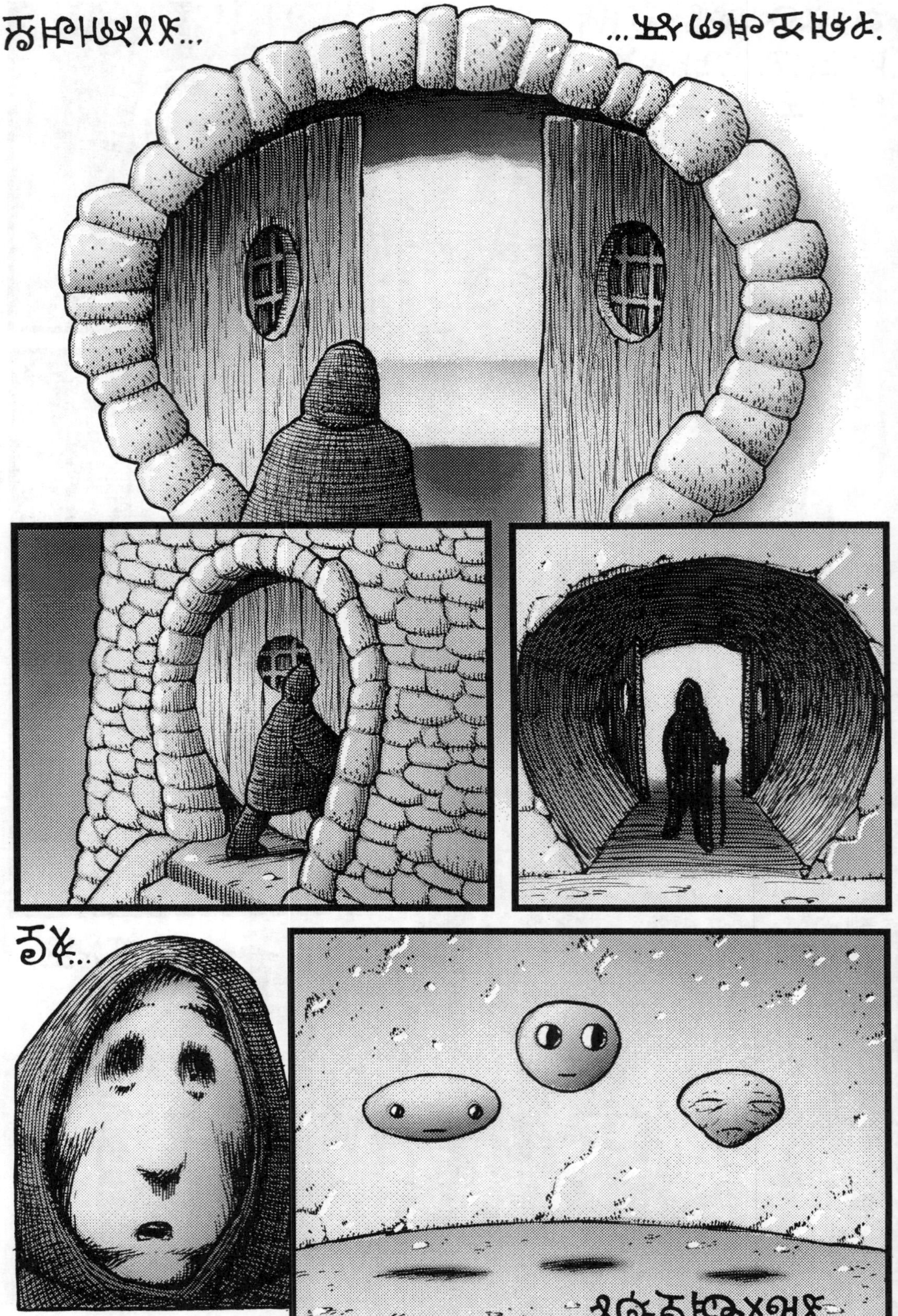

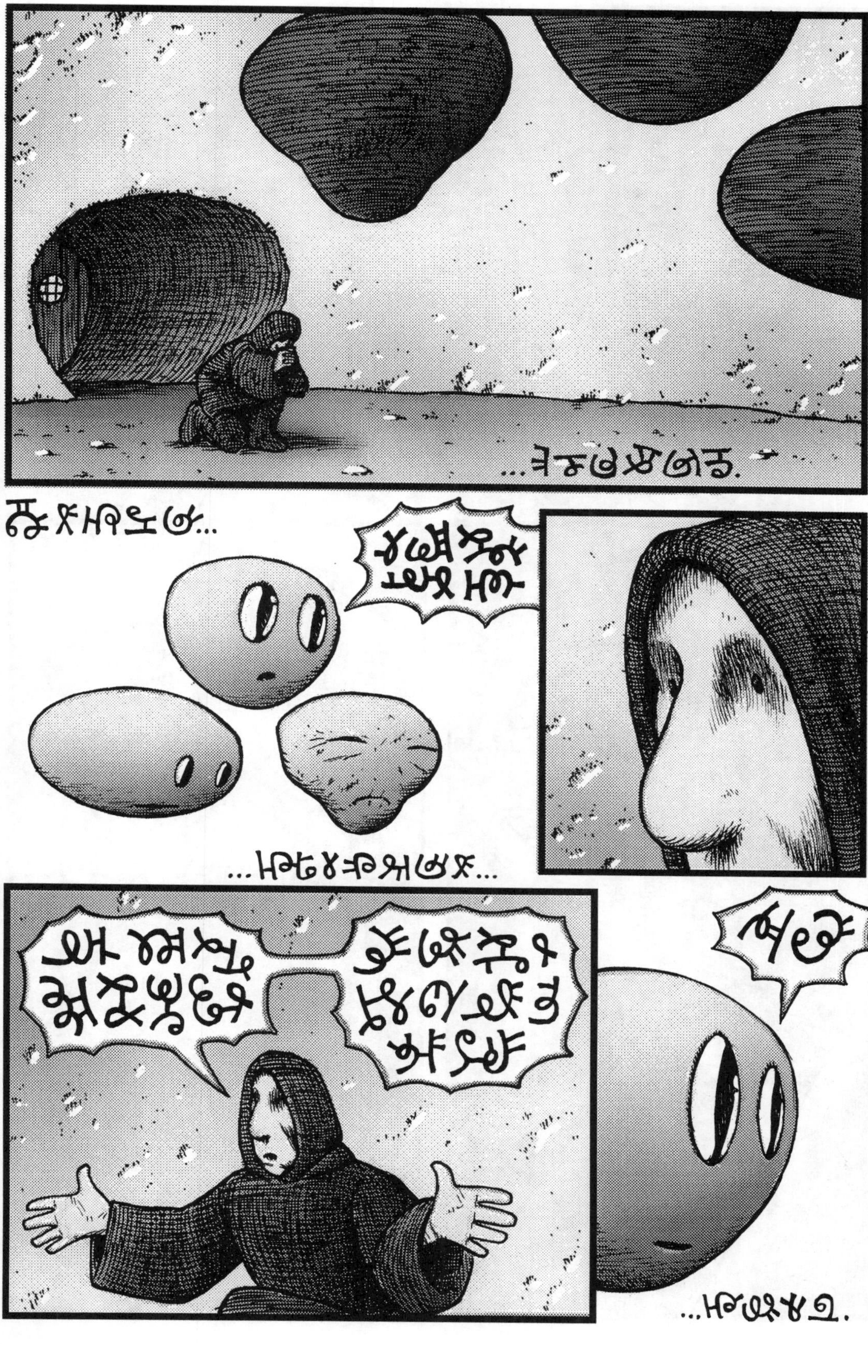

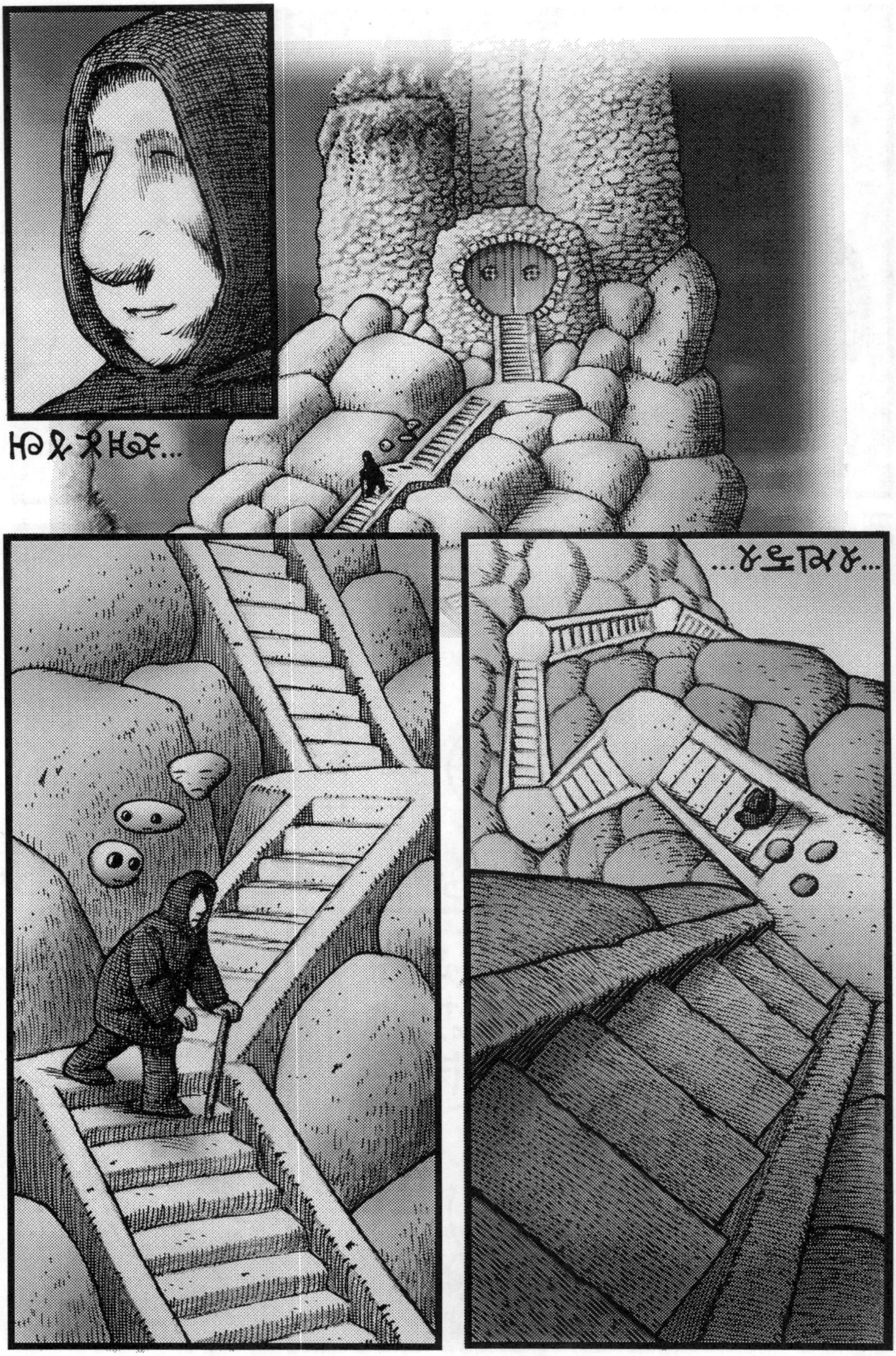

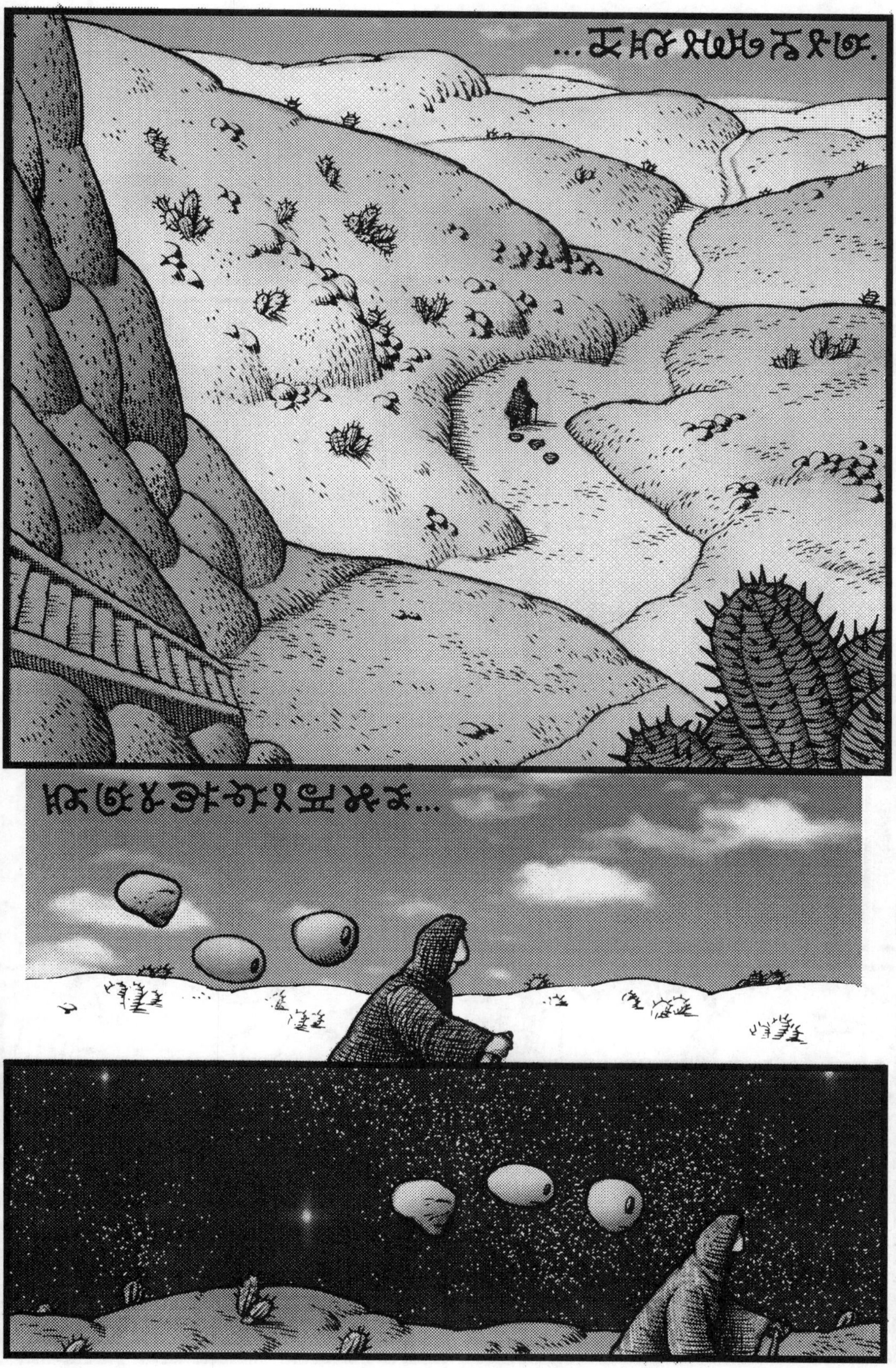

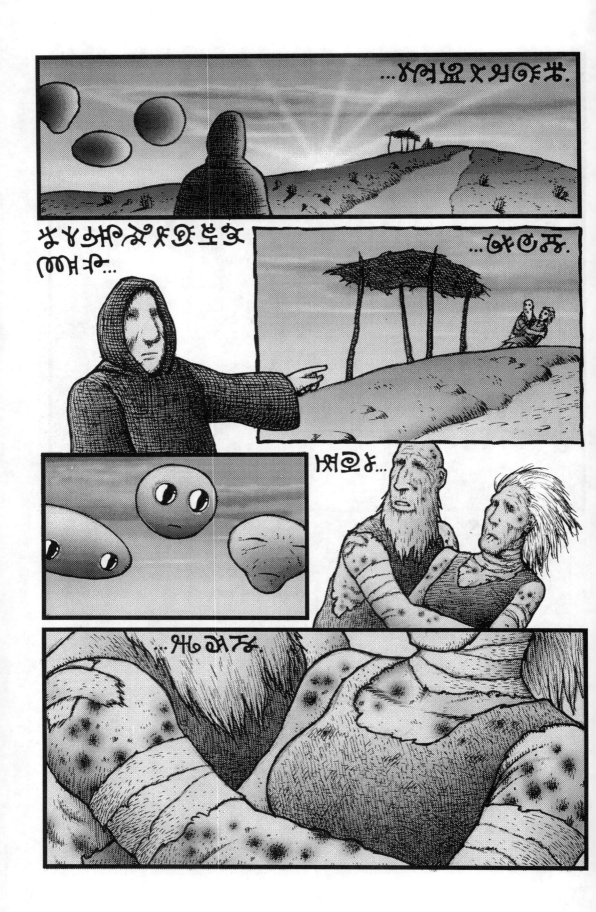

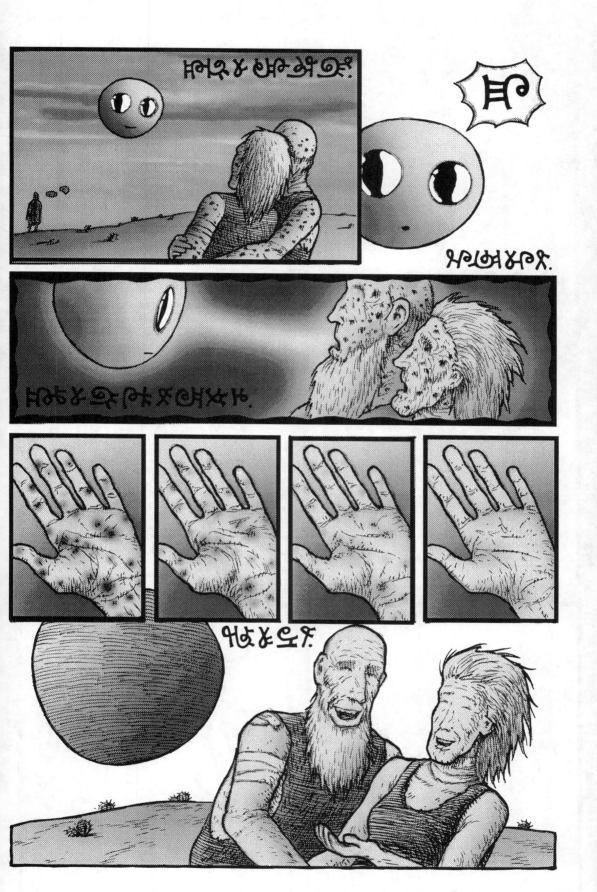

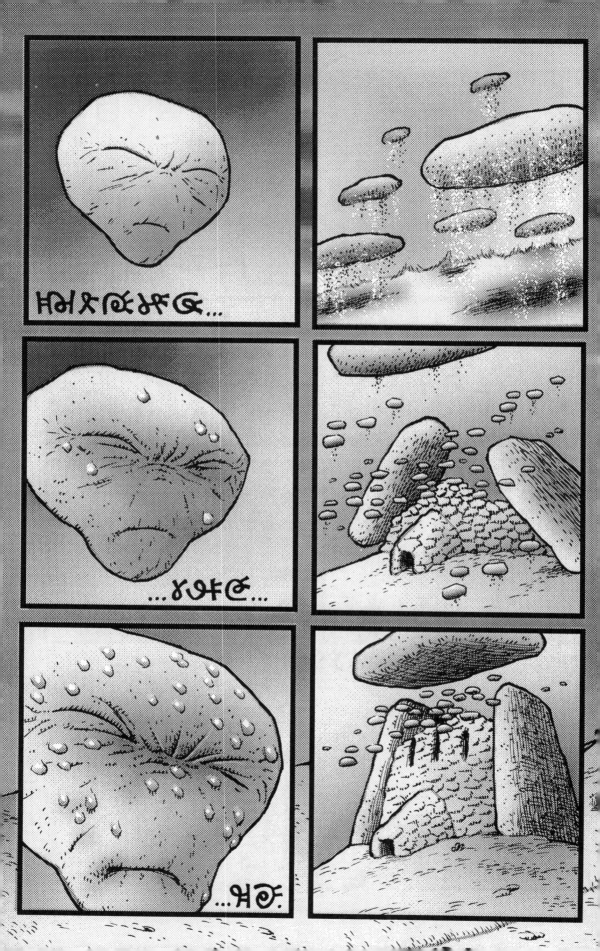

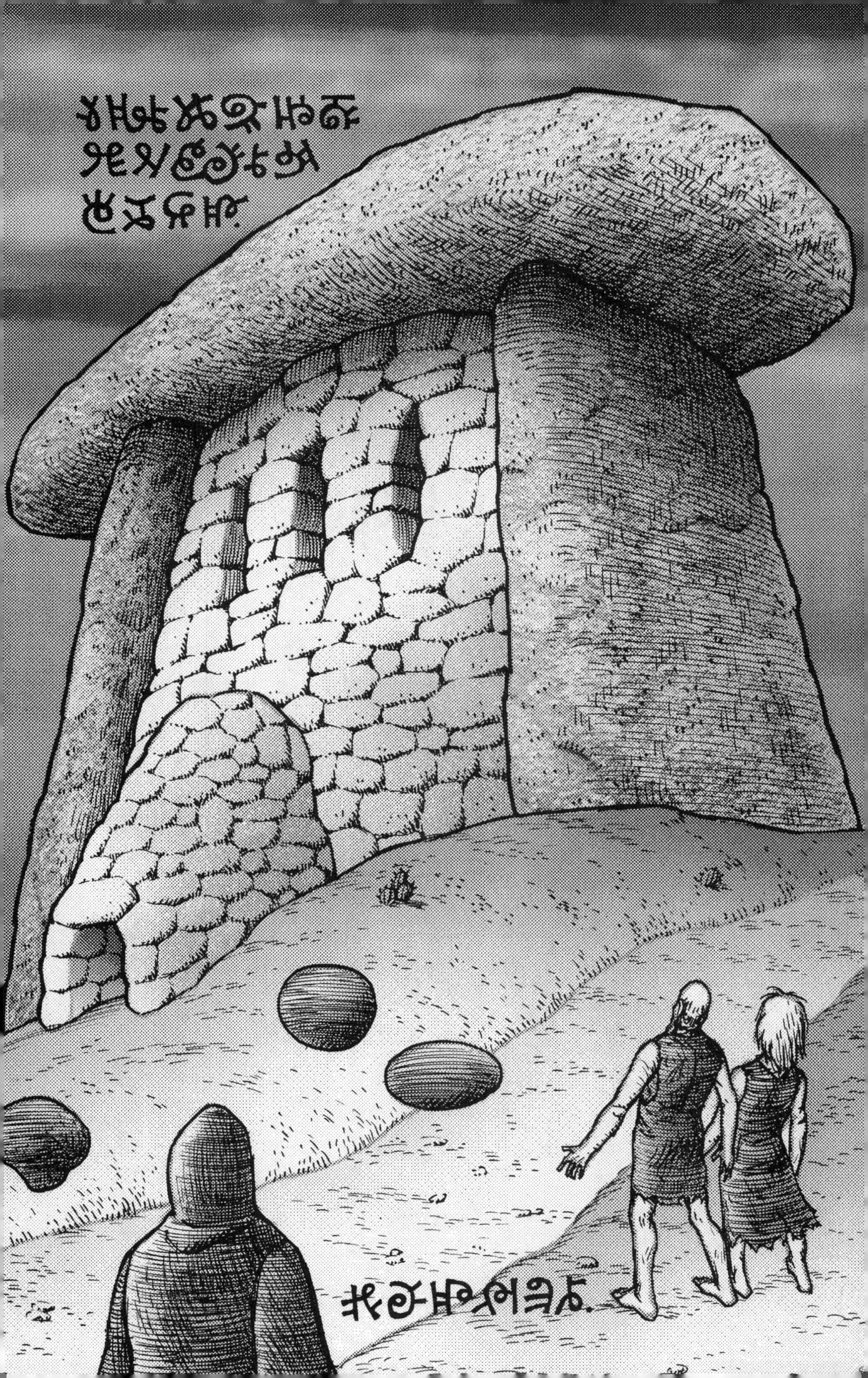

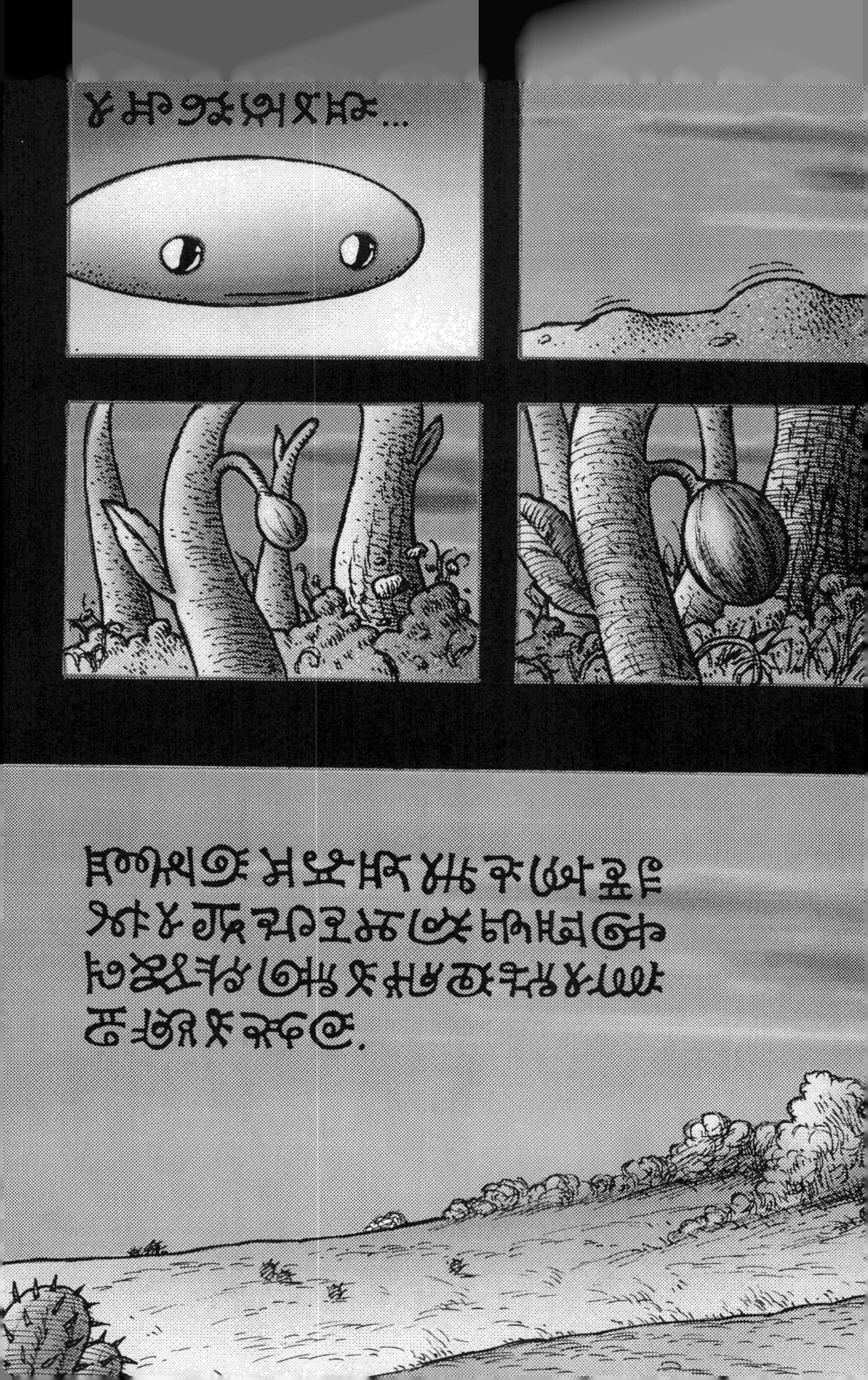

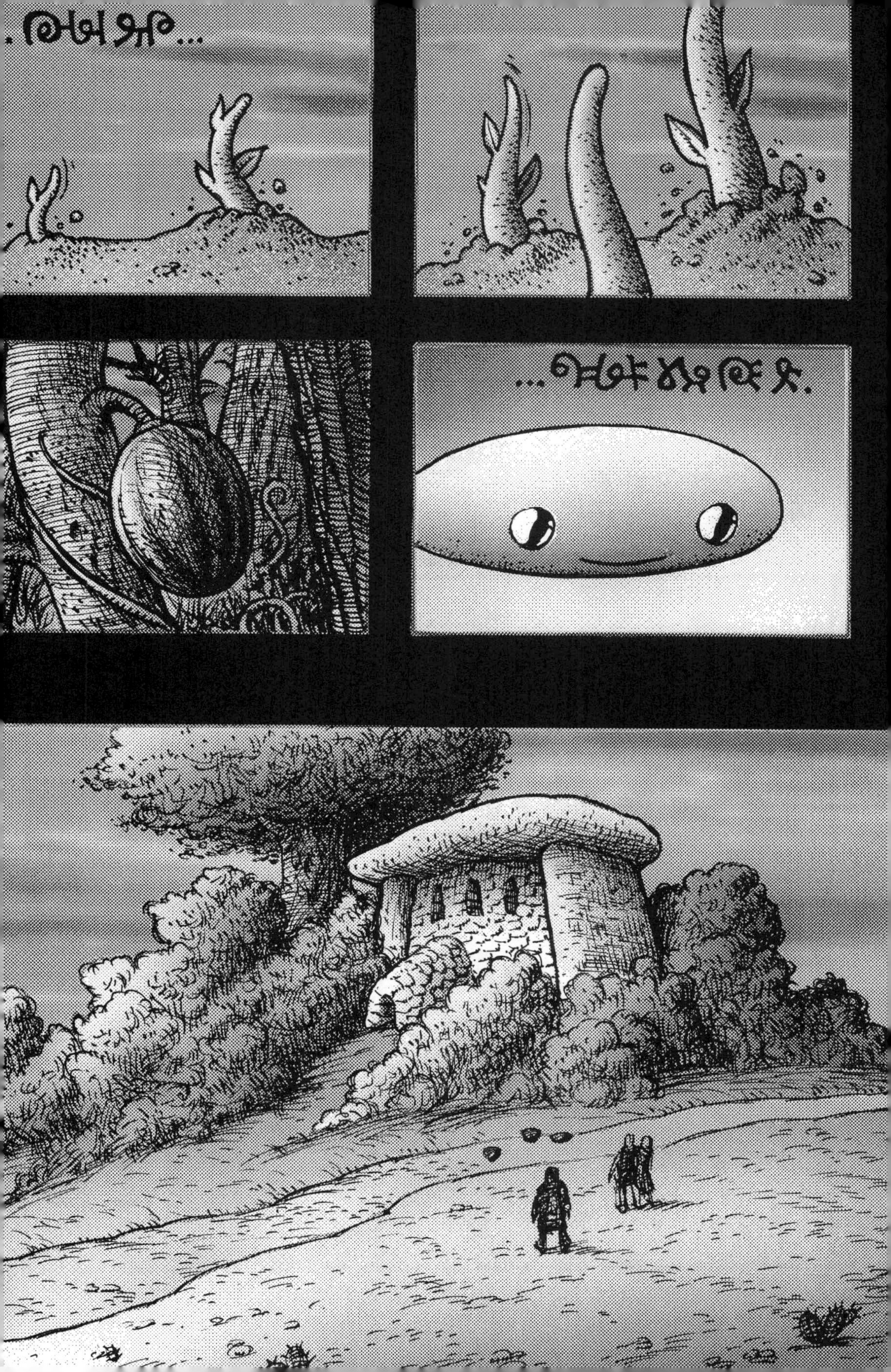

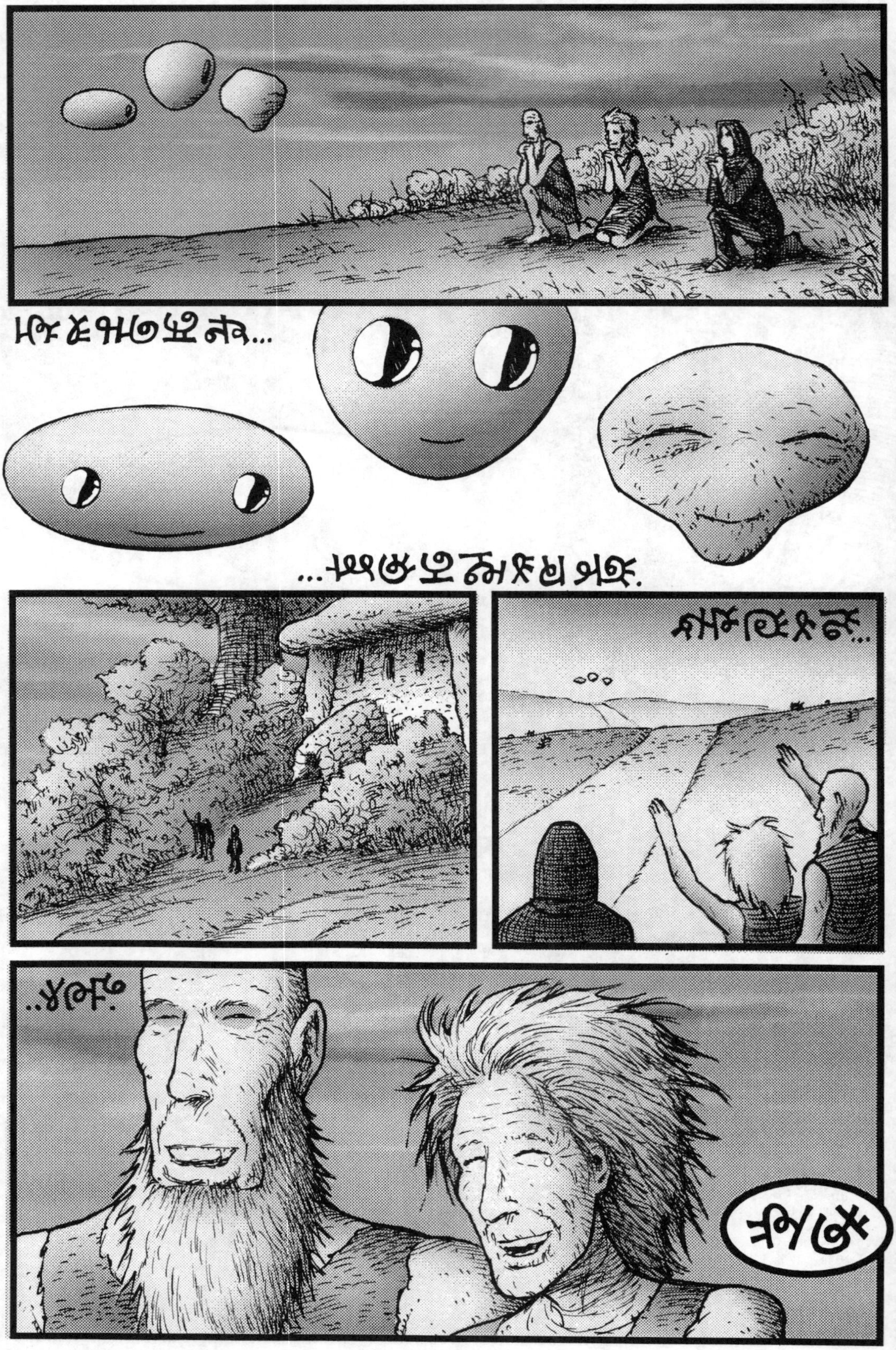

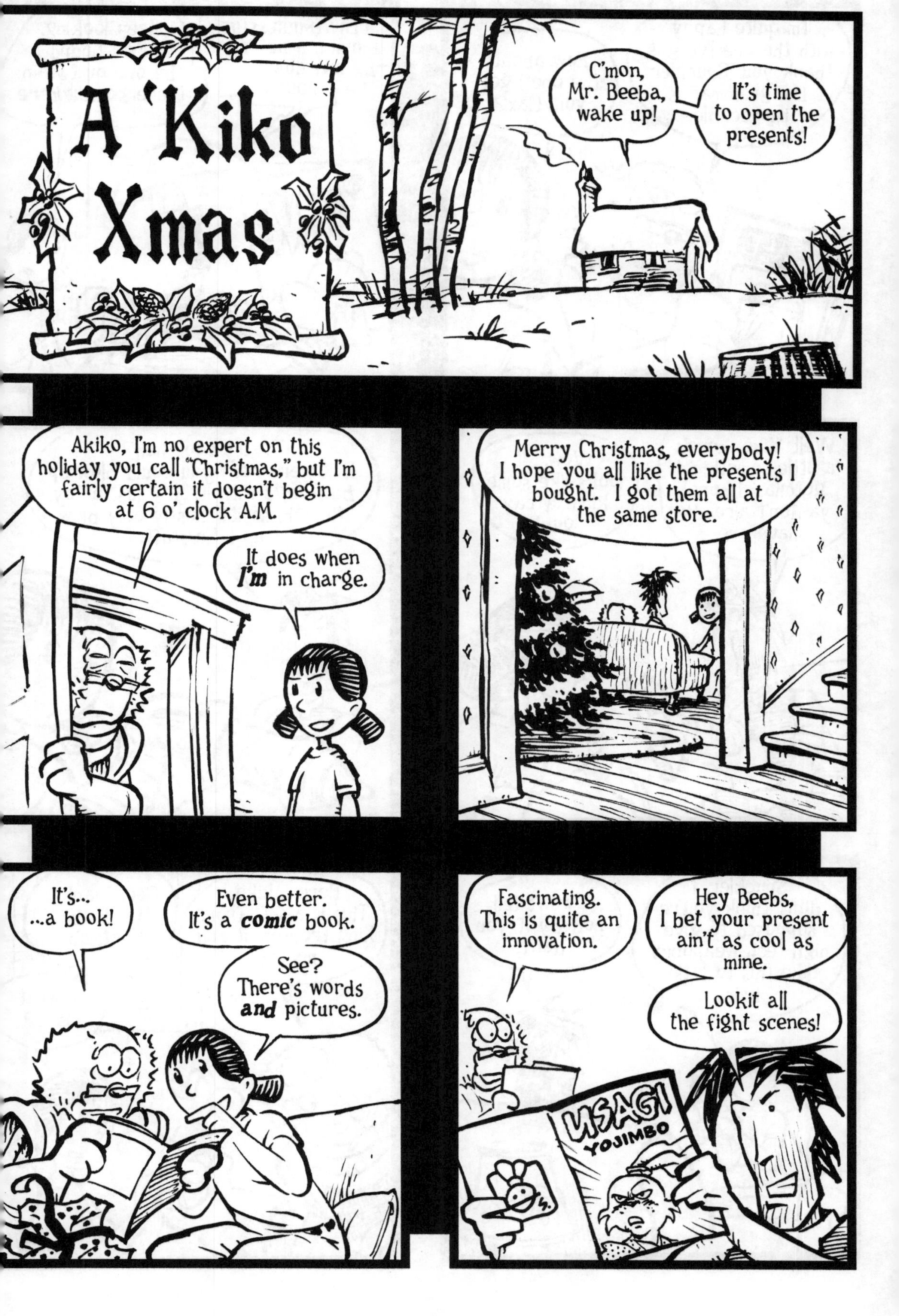
A 'Kiko Xmas
C'mon, Mr. Beeba, wake up!
It's time to open the presents!
Akiko, I'm no expert on this holiday you call "Christmas," but I'm fairly certain it doesn't begin at 6 o' clock A.M.
It does when *I'm* in charge.
Merry Christmas, everybody! I hope you all like the presents I bought. I got them all at the same store.
It's... ...a book!
Even better. It's a **comic** book.
See? There's words **and** pictures.
Fascinating. This is quite an innovation.
Hey Beebs, I bet your present ain't as cool as mine.
Lookit all the fight scenes!
USAGI YOJIMBO

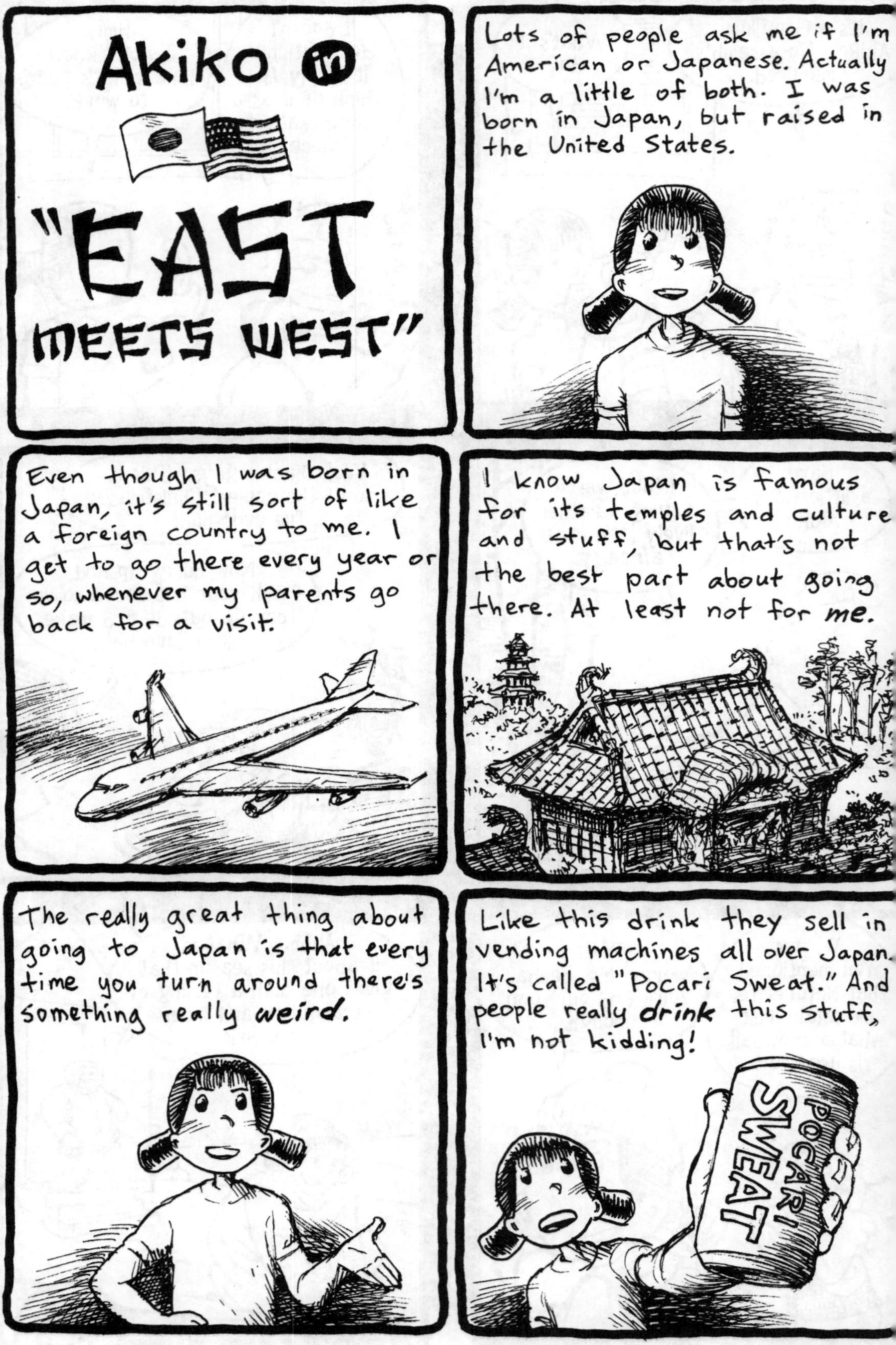
Akiko in
"EAST MEETS WEST"
Lots of people ask me if I'm American or Japanese. Actually I'm a little of both. I was born in Japan, but raised in the United States.
Even though I was born in Japan, it's still sort of like a foreign country to me. I get to go there every year or so, whenever my parents go back for a visit.
I know Japan is famous for its temples and culture and stuff, but that's not the best part about going there. At least not for me.
The really great thing about going to Japan is that every time you turn around there's something really weird.
Like this drink they sell in vending machines all over Japan. It's called "Pocari Sweat." And people really drink this stuff, I'm not kidding!
POCARI SWEAT

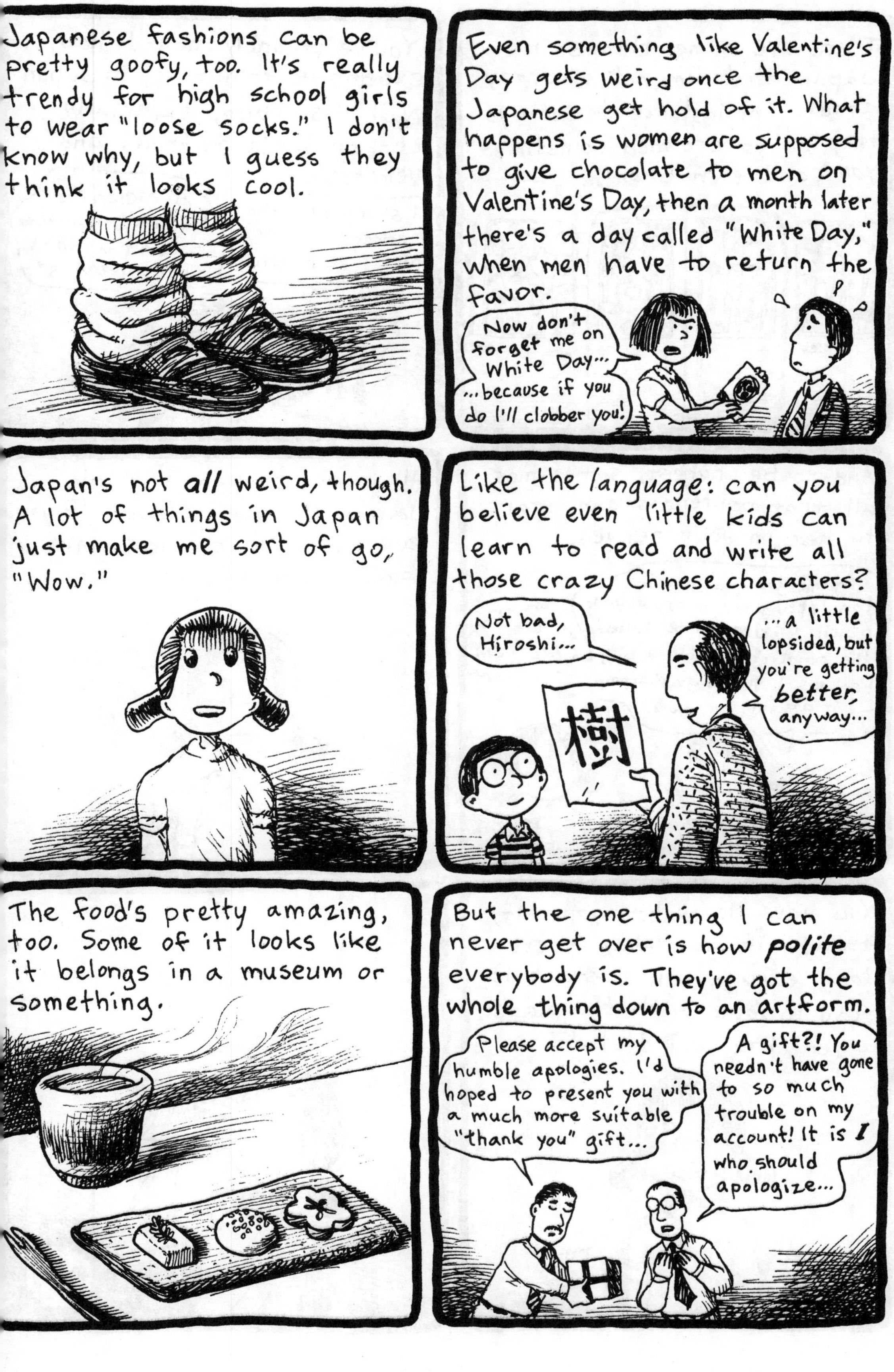
Japanese fashions can be pretty goofy, too. It's really trendy for high school girls to wear "loose socks." I don't know why, but I guess they think it looks cool.
Even something like Valentine's Day gets weird once the Japanese get hold of it. What happens is women are supposed to give chocolate to men on Valentine's Day, then a month later there's a day called "White Day," when men have to return the favor.
Now don't forget me on White Day...
...because if you do I'll clobber you!
Japan's not *all* weird, though. A lot of things in Japan just make me sort of go, "Wow."
Like the *language*: can you believe even little kids can learn to read and write all those crazy Chinese characters?
Not bad, Hiroshi...
樹
...a little lopsided, but you're getting *better*, anyway...
The food's pretty amazing, too. Some of it looks like it belongs in a museum or something.
But the one thing I can never get over is how *polite* everybody is. They've got the whole thing down to an artform.
Please accept my humble apologies. I'd hoped to present you with a much more suitable "thank you" gift...
A gift?! You needn't have gone to so much trouble on my account! It is *I* who should apologize...

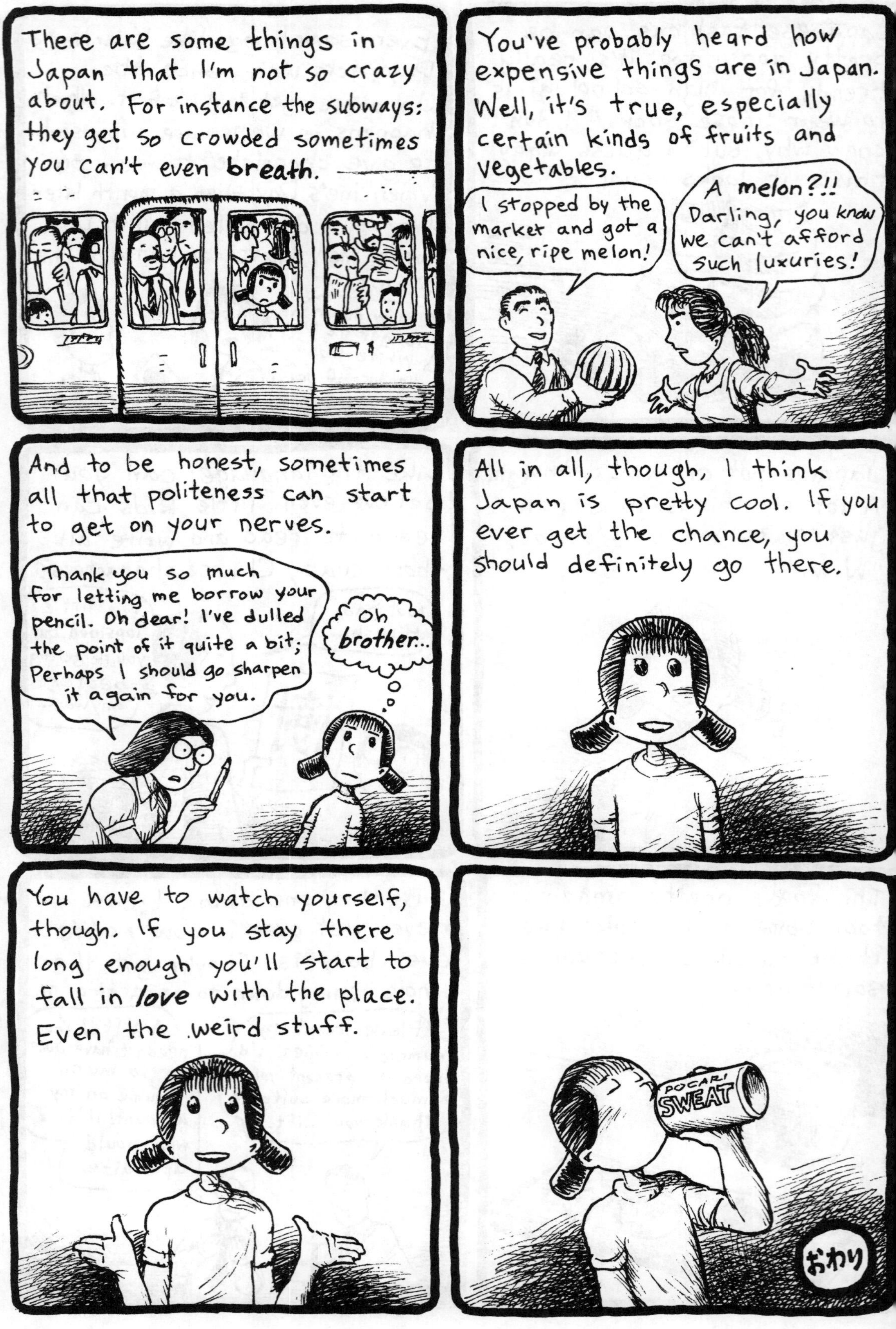
There are some things in Japan that I'm not so crazy about. For instance the subways: they get so crowded sometimes you can't even **breath**.
You've probably heard how expensive things are in Japan. Well, it's true, especially certain kinds of fruits and vegetables.
I stopped by the market and got a nice, ripe melon!
A **melon**?!! Darling, you know we can't afford such luxuries!
And to be honest, sometimes all that politeness can start to get on your nerves.
Thank you so much for letting me borrow your pencil. Oh dear! I've dulled the point of it quite a bit; Perhaps I should go sharpen it again for you.
Oh **brother**...
All in all, though, I think Japan is pretty cool. If you ever get the chance, you should definitely go there.
You have to watch yourself, though. If you stay there long enough you'll start to fall in ***love*** with the place. Even the weird stuff.
POCARI SWEAT
おわり

TWENTY FOUR WAYS TO DRAW POOG

Celtic Poog

Siamese Poogs

Batpoog

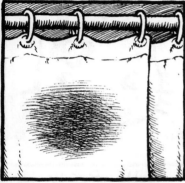

Shower Scene Poog

The Poog in the Hat

Cyber Poog

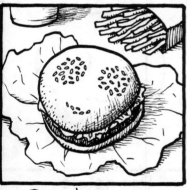

Poogburger

Poog Sushi

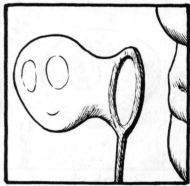

Poog Bubble

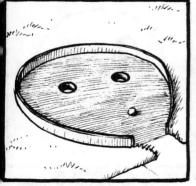

Putt-Putt Poog

Country Poog

Gorbachev Poog

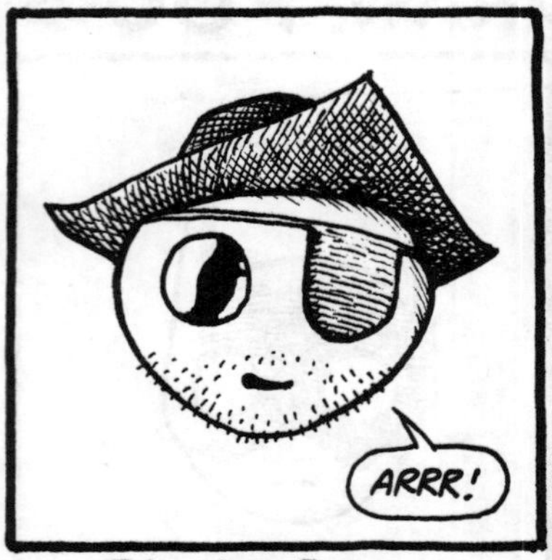
ARRR!

Pirate Poog

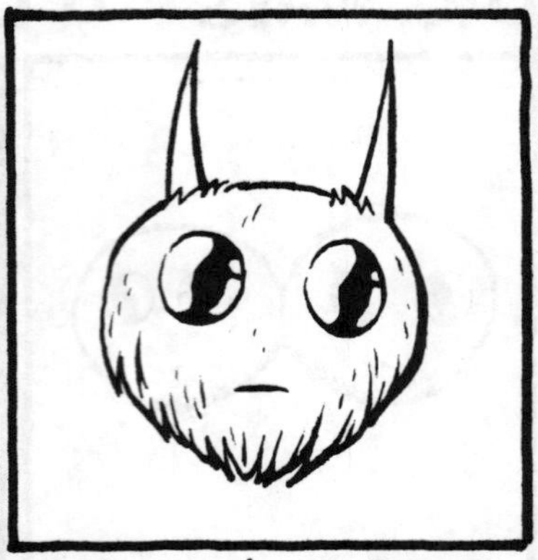

Rat Creature Poog

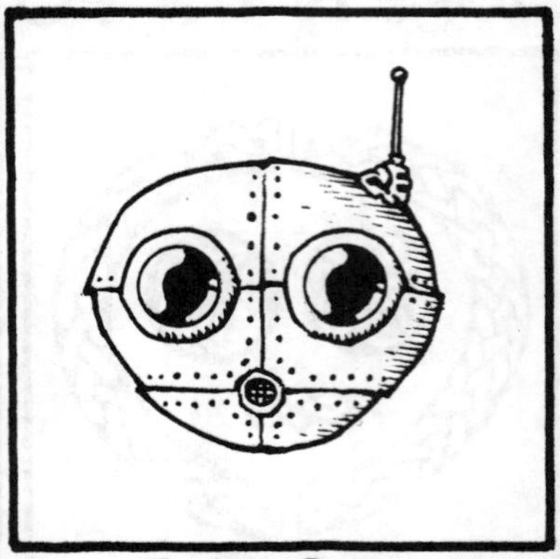

Robo-Poog

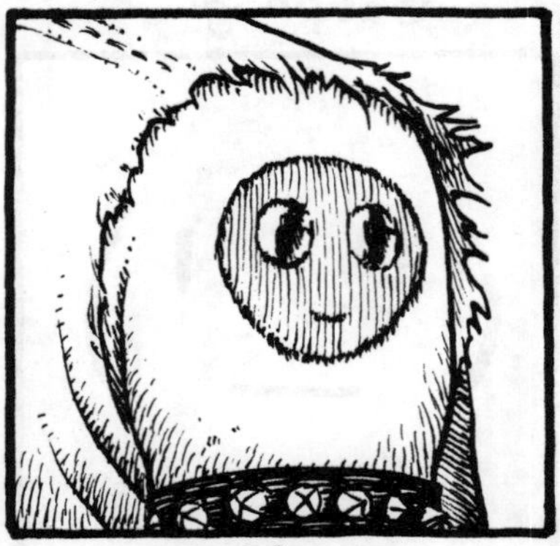

Tattoog

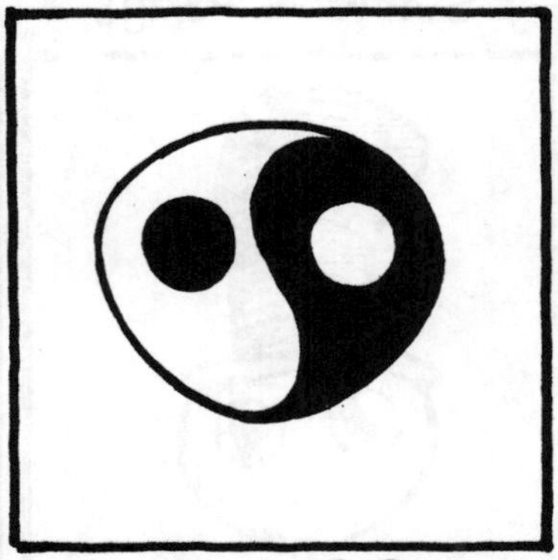

The Tao of Poog

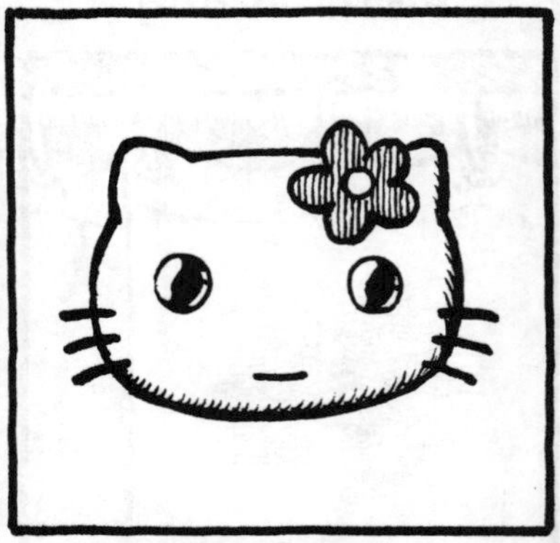

Hello Poogy

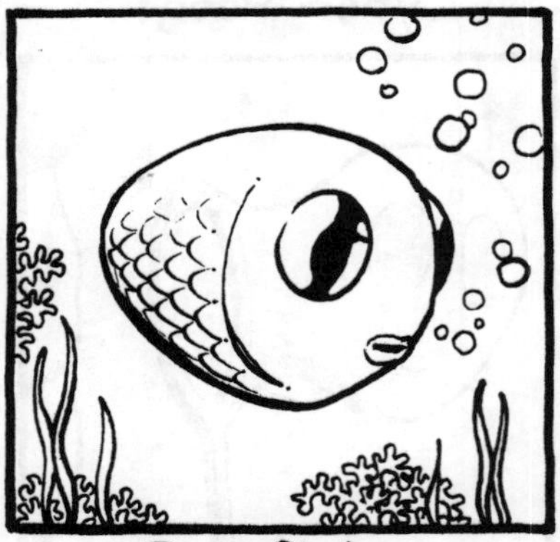

Poogfish

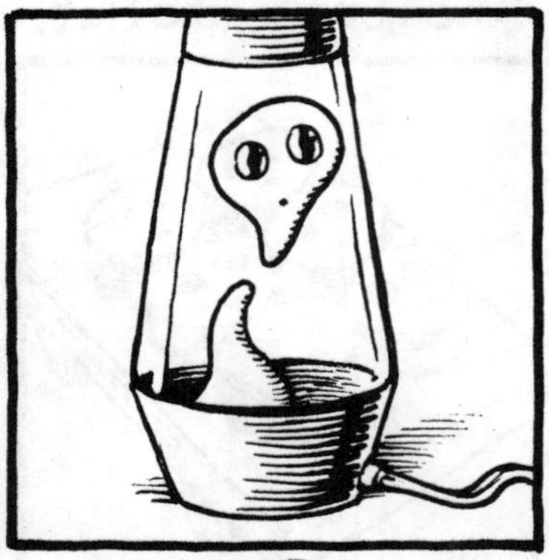

Lava Poog

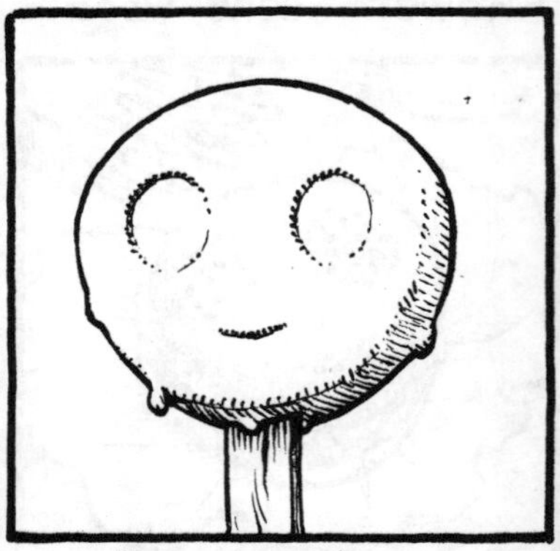

Poogsicle

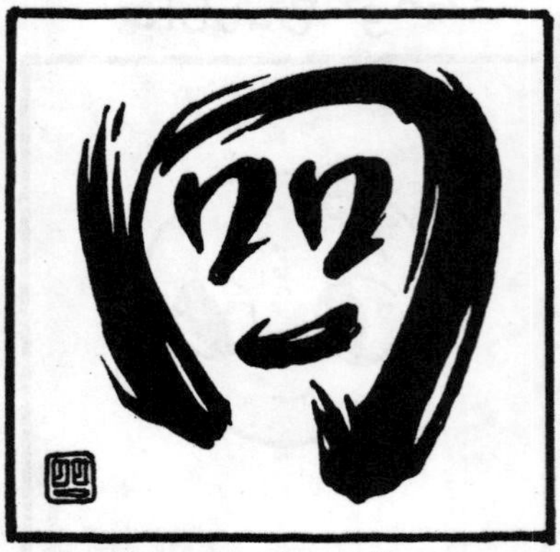

Calligraphy Poog

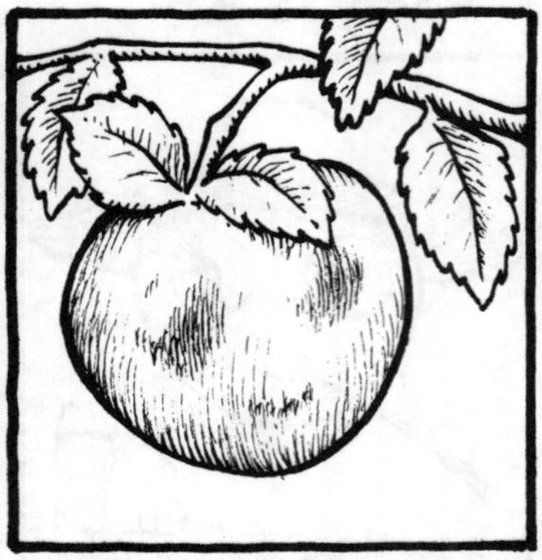

Organic Poog

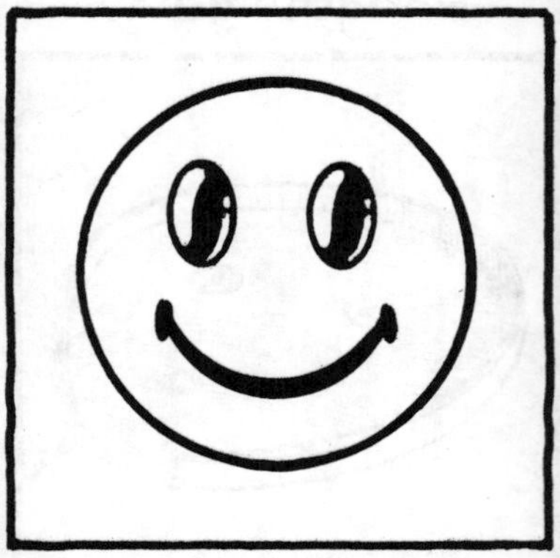

Have a Nice Poog